Praying for Your Family

An Eternal Legacy

SAMMY TIPPIT

Copyright 2006 by Sammy Tippit

All rights reserved. Written permission must be secured from the publisher to use or reproduce any part of this book – except for brief quotations in critical reviews or articles.

Published in 2006 by Sammy Tippit Ministries

Reprinted by Sammy Tippit Books and CreateSpace 2015

Scripture quotations noted NASB are from the NEW AMERICAN STANDARD BIBLE (registration mark needed), Copyright The Lockman Foundation 1960, 1962, 1963, 1968, 1971, 1972, 1973, 1975, 1977. Used by permission.

Library of Congress Cataloging-in-Publication Data

Tippit, Sammy. Praying for Your Family: An Eternal Legacy / Sammy Tippit.

ISBN: 978-0-9864411-2-7

Printed in the United States of America.

In memory of Eliza Bass Tippit – the praying grandmother who I never met but who set the course of my life through her prayers.

In appreciation: I give many thanks to my cousin Jane Parker McManus for all of the research she has done on our family's history. Her research enabled me to learn the "Prayer Legacy" that has been left to me. I also appreciate the "Redbone Heritage Foundation" for all of the research they have done into the people group known as "Redbones" from which I descend. I also am indebted to the Louisiana Baptist Convention for materials that they provided me that helped me with my research. I thank my lifelong prayer partner – my wife Tex. She has traveled with me on this exciting journey of prayer for more than four decades. Most of all, I give thanks and glory to the God who continues to answer the prayers of His people throughout every generation.

CONTENTS

Introduction	Page 1
Chapter One - The Meeting Place	Page 7
Chapter Two - Praying for Your Family	Page 25
Chapter Three - Praying for Your Children	Page 43
Chapter Four - Praying with a Forgiving Heart	Page 65
Chapter Five - Tearing Down Strongholds	Page 83
Chapter Six - Desperate Praying	Page 99
Chapter Seven - Leaving a Legacy	Page 115
Endnotes	Page 133
Information & Resources	Page 136

Introduction

For most people present at the conference, it was a moving moment. For me, it was somewhat different – a revelation. The auditorium at the Billy Graham Training Center at the Cove in Asheville, North Carolina was filled to capacity with pastors and church leaders who had a passion to see spiritual awakening. I had spoken the previous day, and a great sense of brokenness engulfed the meeting. Yet I was unprepared for what transpired after Jim Cymbala, pastor of The Brooklyn Tabernacle in New York City, spoke. Pastor Cymbala told the story of his daughter – how she walked away from God during her teen years. He described how he and his wife cried out to God for her and then watched God work miraculously to bring her back to Himself. At the close of his message, he invited those with wayward children or grandchildren to come to the front of the auditorium so that we could pray for them. As people flocked to the front of the auditorium, I was completely taken by surprise. Almost all of those attending the conference responded, crying out to God for their families.

I was not surprised at how many people had children or grandchildren who had forsaken the God of their fathers, but I was amazed that it was such a high percentage. Those attending the conference were men and women with a genuine heart cry for revival in our nation – people with a deep love for the Savior. They were the *crème de la crème* among God's servants. Yet the vast majority of them were hurting deeply. There had been a time when I would have been standing among them. However, several years earlier, my wife and I experienced a similar miracle to Pastor Cymbala. We watched God work in our children's lives to bring them back to Himself.

As Pastor Cymbala prayed with the people, my heart cried to God for a mighty revival. However, this time I directed my prayer somewhat differently from most other times when I have asked God to revive our nation. I realized that perhaps the greatest felt need among Christians in our nation lies within our families. The family has been under attack for several generations, wounding many of our children and grandchildren in the battle. In that moment at the Cove, I recognized there is an urgency to kneel down, cry to God, and win the battle for future generations. The Apostle Paul, under the inspiration of the Holy Spirit, wrote that our battle is not against flesh and blood, but against principalities and powers from on high. The battle for our children and grandchildren will be won or lost by tears we sow into the soil of their lives through our heartfelt prayers.

I did not come to this conclusion in any ordinary manner. I wish I could tell you my conclusions came from extensive research on the subject of prayer. In 1987, I wrote a book titled *The Prayer Factor*, which was translated into nearly twenty languages. That book has been the number-one resource we have used in our international evangelistic ministry. However, recent events in my life have brought me to a new level of understanding of the power of prayer. I have become convinced that prayer is both the great mystery and the mighty weapon of the believing Christian. It not only has the power to shape our lives but the lives of people who we will never meet on this side of heaven.

A few months before embarking upon writing this manuscript, a number of events, which I will describe in the following pages, radically altered my life. Almost everything I believed about myself was shaken to the core. Through a strange set of circumstances, I became aware of my heritage. I learned my roots come from an unknown group of people in the piney woods of Louisiana. One historical researcher has referred to them as "Louisiana's mystery people." They were the people who God chose to launch Protestant Christianity west of the Mississippi River. They were a mixed race of people with a violent history.[1] However, God sent the son of an Indian slave and a handful of people, who were also of this mixed race, as His ambassadors to the land of bayous. They crossed the cultural divide and proclaimed the gospel. Ultimately, these "mystery people," in part, birthed the Louisiana Baptist Convention.[2]

The great-granddaughter of one of those original Christian pioneers into Louisiana died five years before I was born, but she would make an impact on my life that would reverberate around the world and touch millions of lives in more than eighty nations. She learned to seek God for her family in those piney forests. Her godly prayers would pave the way for me to walk into a revolution in Romania, the aftermath of genocide in Rwanda, and preach the good news of God's love in the middle of wars. I would not have any idea about the impact of her life on mine until sixty-three years after she died. She would not have any idea either – until she reached heaven's gates.

That woman owned little but possessed much. That dear woman, a descendant of a mixed race, possessed something far richer than any material thing this world could offer her. She inherited a legacy given to her by a long line of praying men and women. She met God in the piney woods of central Louisiana, and millions of people in the darkest parts of the world have felt the impact of her prayers. She left a legacy – a prayer legacy.

In the following pages, you will read this intriguing story of how God raised up a humble, praying woman in the middle of a mystery people called "Redbones" and used her to affect history and nations that she never imagined. You will discover that prayer is the place where the sovereignty of God and the will of man intersect. You will learn how you can leave a legacy with your children and grandchildren – a legacy of prayer. You will read about the great heroes of the faith – people in the Bible and people throughout history who have prayed and then watched God do extraordinary things. You will see they were common, ordinary men and women who simply learned to wait upon God.

You will discover you were left a legacy and you too can leave one – a prayer legacy. You will learn principles that will enable you to pray effectively for your children, grandchildren, and even your larger family. You will understand spiritual strongholds and learn how God removes them from your life. You will taste of forgiveness and find the blessing that rests on the sorrows of your family life.

You will learn that Evangelical Christians are still living in the afterglow of an incredible legacy of prayer. A mighty revival swept across North America 150 years prior to the publishing of this manuscript. It was the last Great Awakening on this continent. Historians commonly call it the "Prayer Revival." Prayer meetings swept across the country in a time of a major financial crisis. Then God intervened. The nation shook. The Protestant church awoke. A simple shoe salesman in one of those prayer meetings, D. L. Moody, was catapulted into a ministry that would shake two continents.

We live today in the afterglow of that great move of God's Spirit. It can happen again. God has not changed. His power is still available. There is no energy shortage with God. He is waiting on those who will seek Him. Those who learn to wait upon Him will be "legacy leavers" and "world transformers."

I invite you to join a rising movement of prayer that is rapidly spreading around the world. This invitation does not go out to only the gifted, the powerful, and the wealthy. It goes to struggling moms; aging grandparents; and multitudes of common, ordinary people. It goes to those hurting and suffering.

It is an invitation to the humble of heart and contrite in spirit. It is an invitation to any who will dare to take the step of faith and follow in the footsteps of Jesus. It is an invitation to petition Jesus in the same manner of

His early disciples, "Lord, teach us to pray." Those who take the challenge will stand on the shoulders of those who have left us a legacy, but they also will leave an incredible legacy for future generations.

Chapter One

The Meeting Place

"It happened that while Jesus was praying in a certain place, after He had finished, one of His disciples said to Him, `Lord, teach us to pray just as John also taught his disciples.'"
[Luke 11:1, NASB]

There is an intersection where people gather from every nation, tribe, tongue, and race. Sometimes people have come in groups, and other times they have quietly approached this incredible junction in a very private manner. They have gathered at this corner for centuries – even thousands of years. This crossroads has had many different names: "the secret closet," "the inner chamber," "the prayer meeting," and "quiet time." When Moses went there, they called it "the tent of the meeting."

I think we will discover one day that more history transpired at this meeting place than at any other spot on the planet. It is the place where legacies are left. Pilgrims have traveled two paths to arrive at this crossroads. One is called *"The Sovereignty of God"* and the other *"The Will of Man."* For centuries, theologians and philosophers have debated which might be the best road to travel. My experience, observation, and personal study of history indicate many great men and women have traveled both roads. It is not which road you take that is so important. The meeting place and what transpires when you arrive determine the kind of legacy you leave.

These pilgrims come from different philosophical directions, but there is one thing both groups have in common. The great chorus they have sung when they have arrived has always been: "For Yours is the kingdom and the power and the glory forever" (Matthew 6:13, NASB). They have fallen at the feet of the Savior and cried, "Worthy is the Lamb that was slain to receive power and riches and wisdom and might and honor and glory and blessing" (Revelation 5:12, NASB).

I have ascribed a simple name to that place – *the place of prayer*. Jesus said His church will be called "a house of prayer" (Matthew 21:13, NASB). It is at the intersection of God's sovereignty and man's choices where lives are changed. Entire communities were changed by the great moves of the sovereign Spirit of God that were wrought through humble, holy praying men and women who chose to seek His face.

The meeting place is a place of Divine visitation, a place where hearts are warmed and spirits are renewed. It is the place of revival. It is a place where legacies are birthed and futures are forged. It is the home of the hurting, the soil of those who suffer, and the way of the weak. It is where Jesus promised He would be among them when two or three gathered in His Name. The meeting place is where the believer experiences the manifest presence of Jesus. Once people enter into the meeting place, they are destined to exit differently.

Something awesome transpires when God's *Sovereignty* intersects with *Man's Will* and the two become one. When one seeks God at that crossroads, nothing is impossible. The Bible says, "This is the confidence which we have before Him, that, if we ask anything according to His will, He hears us. And if we know that He hears us in whatever we ask, we know that we have the requests which we have asked from Him" (1 John 5:14-15, NASB). It is the combination of His will and our asking that releases the Spirit of God to do far above all that we could ask or even think about asking.

The meeting place is the corner where the will of man intersects the sovereignty of God. As they cross, people worship Christ and lives are transformed. The sovereignty of God says, ". . . Apart from Me you can do nothing" (John 15:5, NASB); while the will of man says, "I can do all things through Him who strengthens me" (Philippians 4:13, NASB). When we go to the meeting place, the sovereignty of God and the will of man come together and there is only one conclusion to be drawn: He is the sole ruler in the affairs of our lives. He is in charge of where we come from and where we are headed. He alone has the power to direct our lives. Those who have learned to place themselves at His disposal ultimately will see the practical outworking of His Spirit in their lives. Those who place their lives in Christ's care know the might of His power working in their lives, families, and world.

For many years, I have known we see God's power most clearly as we learn to pray; but recently, that truth became more real than I had ever imagined. I have known that life is naturally full of surprises. However, when we seek Christ in prayer, the surprises become bigger and more filled with wonder and awe than we ever dreamed. One of the greatest surprises of my life led me to understand how this meeting place is at the corner of *God's Sovereignty* and *Man's Will*. This surprise came as suddenly as a bolt of lightning on a stormy night. It came when my sister called and said, "Sammy, we may have a brother who we never knew about; and he lives in Portugal."

A man who grew up in Britain, retired early, and was living near a golf resort off the coast of Portugal made contact with my sister, saying he had evidence he was our brother and he had DNA evidence that we came from the same Indian tribe. As he told me his story, my heart sank. The implication was that my father and his mother had a relationship during World War II, making him my half brother. His mother committed suicide in 1963, and he tied her death to her relationship with my father. Confusion filled my mind as I heard his story.

To say the least, all of this took me by surprise. Questions flooded my heart like a tsunami suddenly rising from the sea. Could my father's actions – or lack of taking responsibility for his actions – have been the cause of the suicide of another person and the emotional trauma of an entire family? On the other hand, was I being disloyal to my father's memory by even thinking that to be possible?

Furthermore, I had no idea I had Indian heritage. I had heard that an ancestor had married an Indian somewhere in my family's history, but that was all. This man knew more about my family than I did. My father became very ill when I was a small child and died when I was in college. It was as though he went into a shell and hid in it when he became ill. My grandparents on my father's side of the family died before I was born, and my grandparents on my mother's side died when I was a preschool child. They had lived in the piney forests of central and southwest Louisiana. I grew up in the city. Thus, I knew very little about my family's history. I was fine with that – until talked to the man living in Portugal.

Questions filled my heart – questions that ultimately would lead me to the meeting place – the corner of the *Sovereignty of God* and the *Will of Man*. "Could my father have birthed a child and then forsaken his responsibility? Who was I? What were my roots? The answers to those questions not only would define my father's legacy but also would define my race, heritage, and identity.

I knew there was only one way to resolve the issue – submit to DNA testing with the man from Portugal. We both agreed to "siblingship" tests. It took three long weeks before the results came back. When I learned we were **not** brothers, relief swept over me when I learned my father was not responsible for the agony of another family. However, the experience left me with a passion to know who I am and where I came from – something that never seemed important before that time.

That longing to know my roots led me to a new understanding of the meeting place. It was God's way of bringing me to understand that history is ***His story***. Yet intertwined with ***His story*** is ***our story*** – yours and mine. The history of nations and peoples is simply the interlacing of God's sovereignty with the daily decisions of common, ordinary people. It helped me to recognize the sovereignty of God and appreciate His Divine plan throughout history. I came to a keen realization that history is not accidental. God has a sovereign plan that is connected directly to our daily decisions. My research also led me to understand why cross-cultural ministry came so naturally to me. Most of all, it caused me to appreciate the "meeting place," a place that was planted in my spiritual DNA long before I was born.

As I researched my roots, I discovered I did come from an Indian heritage. My third-great grandfather migrated from North Carolina to Louisiana about the time of the Louisiana Purchase and settled there. [1] He descended from a mixed race of people with a unique culture and lived among other people of the same racial mixture which historians call "Louisiana Redbones." He was instrumental in assisting in the formation of some of Louisiana's first Protestant churches and perhaps the very first Baptist church west of the Mississippi River. [2] This passion for God was passed down to his children and grandchildren. His great-granddaughter Eliza Jane Bass married Samuel Clinton Tippit. They were the grandparents who I never knew but have now come to love and appreciate.

My grandmother had been simply a person in my family history who I had heard about. When I discovered the legacy she left me, I was able to say for the first time, "I love my grandmother." I had a new appreciation for her and the "meeting place" where she encountered God. I never knew I had any kind of Christian heritage. I had never known that my grandparents a few generations back would be at the foundation of a major denomination in Louisiana. I had no idea that my grandmother was a mighty woman of prayer. However, I began to learn that my passion to see a mighty, sweeping revival was in my spiritual DNA. My grandmother prayed, and a grandson who never knew her reaped the benefits of her prayers more than a quarter of a century later.

I knew very little about my grandparents, but one of the most incredible things I learned about my grandmother was that she had a place under the trees where she met with God. It was her secret place. A cousin sent me a poem that her mother had written about our grandmother's meeting place. As I began researching my roots, I found a description of my grandmother that my aunt had written: *I think mother felt that she could talk to her Redeemer better in her garden near this peach tree than anywhere else on the farm. So many times, she would steal away and pray, and so many times, it was under a peach tree. When I heard her pray, I knew there was a direct connection between her and God. She would tell Him what she hoped for, and the answer was sure to come.*

Mother was a meek, humble, God-loving person. She lived close to God, loved her church, husband, and children. She totally trusted God for all her needs – I only wish I could describe exactly how she trusted God, but words cannot begin to explain. Her trust was not for just one day, but for every day of her life. [3]

One of the reasons that learning about my grandmother was so mind boggling is I have had a place under the trees where I have gone for the past twenty years. Each morning before going to my office, I get a cup of coffee and go to that meeting place. To everyone else, it is just an ordinary clump of trees. However, to me, it is holy ground. I have shared my deepest sorrows and greatest joys with the One who created me in that place. For decades, my meeting place has been under the trees – just as it was for the grandmother who I never knew.

I grew up thinking I had no Christian heritage. My parents very seldom attended church. When I placed my faith in Christ as a university student, Mom did not understand. My parents cared about me and sacrificed so much to give me an opportunity to achieve in life. We did not have much materially, but they always encouraged me. However, there were two major problems that Mom had with my new faith. God called me to preach, and I began to love people of other races. Mom did not understand either of those life changes. Nevertheless, eventually I would learn it was God's way of leading me to enroll in the school of prayer.

There was another thing of great significance that happened after I became a Christian. Not long after coming to Christ, some men from my new church came to our house, read the Bible to my dad, and prayed with him. He asked Christ into his heart, to forgive him, and to take control of his life. Not long after that encounter with God, Dad went to be with the God he had come to love.

After learning about my grandmother, I realized she died not having seen the answer to her prayers for my dad. Yet twenty-three years after her death, God reached down and saved her grandson – a grandchild who she never met. Two years after that, her grandson's life would be used of God to bring her son to Christ. As I came to this realization, I wept. "Oh, God," I cried. "You are Sovereign. You answer the prayers of Your people in ways that are so far beyond our imagination." Everyone in my family has given their lives to Christ since that time. It all began with a praying grandmother who I never knew and a prayer legacy passed down to our family.

When I realized the pattern set for me through a praying grandmother, I understood why prayer has played such an important role throughout my Christian life. Early in my walk with God, I began meeting with some friends near the State Capitol building in Baton Rouge, Louisiana. We would rise early in the morning, go to that quiet spot near the capitol, and spend time in prayer and reading the Scriptures. No one told us to do that. It was natural. When I visit Baton Rouge, I try to go to that spot. After forty years, the fragrance of God's presence remains in that meeting place – under those trees.

A grandmother who I never knew left me a legacy – a legacy of prayer. Since that day, I have proclaimed the Gospel around the world. I have built a ministry rooted in prayer that has touched more than eighty nations. I made a decision early in my ministry not to try to raise finances but rather raise prayer warriors for our ministry. God has blessed in a marvelous way. He has met every need of our ministry, and it has grown to where we have held major evangelistic campaigns around the globe – all of it built on prayer.

You may be thinking, *Oh, that's great for you. However, I'm no one special. I'm not an international evangelist. I'm not some great preacher. I'm simply a Christian with a love for my children and want God's best for them. I live an ordinary life.*

The beauty of my grandmother's life is that she was completely ordinary. Yet she had a place where she met an extraordinary God. She lived in the pine forests of Louisiana. She and her parents were simple farmers. They lived in a community where outsiders spoke derogatorily of their mixed race. Yet she lived with dignity.

The history of the Protestant church and Baptists in Louisiana would not be the same without the fervent prayers and missionary spirit of the "Louisiana Redbones" – Joseph Willis and his companions like John Bass. It amazes me to see how often God uses the ordinary. He took a people with a unique culture and mixed race to help birth the Baptist movement in Louisiana.

When God looks for people He can use, He does not check their racial makeup. He does not look at their resume to see the school from which they graduated. He does not peek at their portfolio. He is simply looking for people who long to know Him and have intimate fellowship with Him. He is seeking the humble of heart, the lowly in spirit, and those longing to know Him intimately. He is not looking at pedigree, position, race, or wealth. He is looking to do the uncommon among the common, the extraordinary among the ordinary.

However, it all begins with a meeting place – a place to steal away and meet with Him, the Lover of your soul. Search the annals of history, and you will discover the leavers of spiritual legacies all had a place – one where they went regularly to meet with the Savior who they loved so dearly. In the Old Testament, you will find Moses pitching a tent outside the camp. There he would go and worship God. In the Gospels, you find Jesus often would find a lonely place and the Son communed with the Father. In the book of Acts, you will find the church gathering in an upper room to wait upon God. In the great spiritual revivals of Christianity, you find the Spirit of God descending upon the wings of a small band of praying men and women.

There probably has not been as great a propagator of the Gospel as the Apostle Paul. When you study his life, you make some very interesting discoveries about prayer. When he went to Philippi, he found a place outside the city near a river and sought God in prayer. (Acts 16:13) Because of going to that special place to pray, a saleslady named Lydia came to Christ and later a slave girl was set free from her spiritual bondage. When the special place was taken away from him and he was thrown in jail, he turned his prison cell into a place of prayer. (Acts 16:25-31) That prayer meeting resulted in the Philippian jailer coming to Christ and opened the possibility for his entire family to do the same.

I wonder what might happen today if a businessperson would find a place among his colleagues and begin to seek God. The times have changed, but God has not. What would happen if a grandmother would steal away to a quiet place and seek God for her children and grandchildren? What impact would it have on future generations? What would happen if Christians around our nation and world would say, "Let's go to the corner, the place where *God's Sovereignty* and *Man's Will* intersect, and join together at the meeting place to seek God."

If we were to commit ourselves to find a place

and a time to meet with God and go to that place with regularity, there is no limit to God's work in our families. Ordinary people, who come to the intersection of *God's Sovereignty* and *Man's Will*, shape history. Common, ordinary people, who commit themselves to making the journey to the meeting place, shape the lives of generations to come.

Moses had a tent where he met God, and that forged the future of the children of Israel. Jesus had a special place of prayer, and it changed the lives of the disciples. The early church had an upper room, and they shook the entire Roman Empire. Paul had a place by the river, and the lives of a woman and a slave girl would never be the same. Jesus told His disciples to "go into your inner room, close your door and pray to your Father who is in secret, and your Father who sees what is done in secret will reward you" (Matthew 6:6, NASB). Legacy leavers are those with a secret place where they meet with God.

You, too, can be a legacy leaver. However, you must first find *a quiet place.* It begins there – a meeting place and a time where you will not be interrupted, a place where you pitch your tent outside the crowds and say, "Lord, teach me to pray." When you find that secret place, generations in the future will each stand at the entrance of their tents and worship God. Heaven's history will record you as a legacy leaver.

Along with that special place, you will need to set aside a time to meet with God. The meeting place requires *a meeting time.* Prayer is ultimately intimacy with God. It is the communion of two hearts – the heart of God and the heart of man. Any good relationship demands honest and open communication. We all have a time for the most important things in life. We have a time to eat, sleep, and go to work. Why not then have a committed time for seeking God in prayer?

When I first met my wife, we fell in love. I will never forget the day she walked down the aisle of the church and said she would love me for the rest of my life. Oh, how I loved her! However, I can honestly say I love her more today than I loved her then. I have spent time with her. We have climbed mountains together and wept with each other in valleys. We have experienced the joy of victory together as well as the depths of sorrow. Love grows with time. When you have that quiet place to meet with God, there will be moments of joy and occasions of sorrow. Yet you will grow in your love for the Savior through it all. That love relationship produces the aroma of a legacy that lasts throughout the generations.

An attorney once asked Jesus what was the greatest commandment of the law. It was an extremely important question. In other words, he wanted to know what one thing God wanted from us. Jesus said it was to love the Lord, our God, with all our heart, soul, mind, and strength. (Mark 12:30 and Luke 10:27) If we are going to do what God created us to do, then we will need to set aside time to commune with the Lover of our soul.

A thief seeks to do everything possible to rob us of that special time alone with God. Its name is "Busyness." It permits us to do many good things to keep us from the great and important things. It normally robs us on the highway of *Man's Will*. God has given all of us an equal amount of time. I may not have as much money or as nice of a home as many people; but God has blessed me with twenty-four hours in one day, the same amount as the wealthiest person in the world. The only question is: "How will I spend that time?"

"Busyness" has a very subtle way of stealing God's best from us. It uses the fun of entertainment, the diligence of hard work, and the rituals of religiosity to keep us from the sweetest and most beautiful moments of our lives. As we travel down the highway called *Man's Will*, we must learn to make choices that lead to time alone with God. If we make choices that enable us to have time with God, we will wake up one day with an incredible discovery. We have come to the place that intersects with *God's Sovereignty*; and at that corner, we will worship as we have never worshipped before. We will fall on our knees and simply cry out, "I love You, Lord."

Because I have a strong work ethic and a desire to serve God with my whole heart, it has been easy for me to sacrifice time alone with Him on the altar of hard work. I found myself doing the work of God and missing the God of the work. That has been the scourge of so many of us in full-time Christian ministry. That has produced burnout in so many of us who long to do His will.

By 1999, our ministry had grown in an incredible way. There was only one explanation for how that happened – God had blessed us. Yet we can easily lose sight of the "Blesser" when we become absorbed with the "Blessing." I preached that year in the national stadium in Addis Ababa, Ethiopia as well as in Maracana, the world's largest stadium in Rio de Janeiro, Brazil. I had longed to share the good news in such venues, and God gave me the desires of my heart.

However, God spoke to my heart in both of those meetings. When I preached the first day in Addis Ababa, people filled the national stadium and were even sitting on the ground. The crowds grew daily until the last day when we would have to have two meetings to accommodate everyone attending. I would preach to more people that day than any other day of my life. When I awoke that day and turned over in the bed to say "good morning" to my wife, no sound came out. I could not believe it. I lost my voice.

I struggled to preach at the stadium that day. Somehow I managed to squeak out the message two times. Hardly anyone could hear me. However, my interpreter was able to understand what I was saying; and his voice was great. I squeaked, he preached, and God blessed. Thousands responded to give their hearts to Christ.

A few months later, I had the opportunity to preach in Rio de Janeiro, Brazil at the world's largest stadium. The governor of the state, the mayor of the city, senators, members of Parliament, and leading pastors were present on the platform with me that day. Halfway through my presentation, I began to squeak again. God was faithful to His Word, and many came to Christ. However, I knew something was wrong.

When I returned to my home in San Antonio, Texas, I went to see a voice specialist. When I awoke that morning, there was a Scripture verse burning in my heart.

The Psalmist wrote, "Cease striving and know that I am God; I will be exalted among the nations, I will be exalted in the earth" (Psalm 46:10, NASB). I could not shake the feeling I had when that Scripture pounded in my soul. I knew God was speaking to me.

The specialist probed my throat to look at my vocal cords and gave me devastating news that day. "You have polyps on your vocal cords," he said. "We will have to do surgery."

That was terrible news to someone who built his entire life around public speaking. I asked if there was any other way we could address the problem without surgery. He hesitantly said I could attempt one thing before we tried the surgery. I would have to remain completely silent for two weeks. He also would give me medication during that period.

My wife and I made a decision that I will never regret. We decided to take the two weeks of silence. We would spend one of them in Arizona at the Grand Canyon. I had never been there, but I had heard that the handiwork of God there is awesome. When we went to the Grand Canyon, I could do nothing but "be still and know that He is God." I decided to read the entire Bible that week. I figured if God was trying to say something to my heart, then I did not want to miss it. However, only one verse kept pounding in my heart – Psalm 46:10, "Cease striving and know that I am God."

God showed me I had become so busy in the work of God that I was beginning to lose my love for the One who had called me to the work. He brought me back to a place – a meeting place. He spoke so forcefully and yet so gently, "Be still and know that I am God." That day I made a choice that I would seek Him above all things, including my ministry. I learned that if I have become so busy that I did not have time for God, then I have become too busy. I needed to rearrange my schedule and make more time to be with the Lover of my soul.

A time and a place. If we are going to leave a legacy with future generations, then we must find that special place and set aside time to meet with Him. If we are going to forge the future of our families, then it is imperative that we have a meeting place and make adequate time to spend with Him.

---

1. Write down your initial thoughts about this chapter.

2. Describe your place of prayer.

3. React to the statement, "It's at the intersection of God's sovereignty and Man's choices where lives are changed." What do you think about this?

4. 1 John 5:14-15 gives you a guarantee. In your own words, summarize that promise and describe what it means to you personally.

5. Read Psalm 78:1-7 and personalize it—make it into your prayer to God.

6. Write out Psalms 46:10.

7. Take a time of silence today and just listen to the One who created the heavens and the earth. What is He saying to you? Write it down.

Chapter Two

Praying for Your Family

"Pray, then, in this way: 'Our Father who is in heaven, Hallowed be Your name.'"
[Matthew 6:9, NASB]

"I'm not a Christian, and I'll never become one. And I don't want you to ever talk to me about this again."

I was stunned when Mom stated her feelings so strongly. What do you do when you cannot talk to your mother about God? I had no other choice. I talked to God about my mother. Yet it seemed so unlikely that Mom would respond. It seemed virtually impossible.

Praying for your family may be the most daunting task you will ever undertake. We find it easier to pray for people who we do not know than to pray for our families. We know the deep problems of those so close to us. We know where they have messed up, and often it seems like an impossible situation. We forget that God specializes in the impossible.

It was easy for me to become discouraged as I prayed for my mom. She was a self-made woman. She taught me I could do anything, go anywhere, and achieve whatever I set my mind to. However, that same strength was what made it so difficult for her to understand what transpired the night I gave my heart to Christ.

I will never forget that night as long as I live. I walked into the Istrouma Baptist Church in Baton Rouge, Louisiana as one person and came out as a completely different person. I had never experienced such love in all of my life. You see, I had a good family, one that cared about my life and future. However, I met Someone that night who loved me like no one had ever loved me. After I prayed and invited Christ into my life, I felt like a ton of bricks lifted from my shoulders. The guilt left me immediately. There was such peace, such joy that filled my heart. I wanted to shout and tell the whole world what happened.

Just one year earlier, I had studied at the United Nations in New York City and been awarded "Most Outstanding Youth Speaker in North America." I traveled around Canada and the United States speaking about peace in the world. However, there was one, small problem. I had no peace in my heart, that is, until Christ came into my life that night.

My first semester at the university was about to begin. I had two academic scholarships to Louisiana State University (LSU), and looked forward to a law degree and involvement in politics. After coming to Christ, I questioned whether that was what I should do. I wanted to take the abilities God had placed within me and share His great love with the whole world.

I talked to the guest speaker at the church that night, and he vividly explained what it took for Jesus to do such a mighty work in my heart. He told me of Jesus' rejection by those whom He loved most. He shared with me how Jesus had been misunderstood and even falsely accused. He told me how He was beaten, tortured, and killed because of His great love for me. The young preacher then looked at me and said, "If Jesus loved you that much, then you ought to be willing to go anywhere, do anything, and tell anyone of that great love – no matter what it costs you."

    I was thrilled at the prospect of serving Christ for the rest of my life. My adrenaline was flowing like a mighty, rushing river. I thought over the speaker's words for two days. Then I knew what I had to do. God had given me special abilities and gifts. I needed to use them for His glory. In my heart, I surrendered my life to full-time Christian ministry. That is when the problems began.

    At that time, my father was dying. No one in his family had ever obtained a university degree. My mother had married a man before meeting my dad. Her first marriage was disastrous because an alcoholic husband abused her. No one in her family had ever attended the university. My brother and sister did not have plans to go to college. My family's future hopes were in my studies at the university. Everyone was saying I could become the governor or a senator.

    Even though my parents did not attend church, I thought Mom and Dad would be excited about my decision. I certainly did not expect their reaction when I told them. "You're going to do what?!" Mom shouted. "After all your dad and I have sacrificed to give you a good education, after we helped you study at the United Nations, after we've done everything for you, you're going to throw away the opportunity to study law to become some preacher? Well, you're not going to live in this house if you're going to be a preacher. You need a psychiatrist. If you're big enough to make such a stupid decision, then you're big enough to live with the consequences," she continued screaming.

I was shattered. I did not know what to do. I went to some of my friends who also had become Christians during the church service and wept. "What do I do?" I asked. "I love my mom and dad, but I really feel this is what God wants me to do." They did not have an answer for me. They just prayed. That seemed to help some. Yet the feelings of rejection ran so deep. Mom was right. They had sacrificed for me. They were there for me to help me do that which they would never be able to do themselves. They had been great parents.

Nevertheless, I could not live their dreams. I had to follow the dreams placed in my heart by God. Then I remembered the words of the guest speaker: "Jesus was rejected and forsaken by those closest to Him." I was hurting so deeply. No one seemed to understand the depth of that hurt, but Jesus did. He had been there. I did not realize how deep the feelings of rejection had run in my heart until I came home one weekend from the university that first year. Mom began screaming that I had destroyed the Tippit name. I was an embarrassment to our family. LSU's daily newspaper had carried a front-page story about me and some friends speaking at "Free Speech Alley." I shared with thousands of students how God had changed my life. I challenged them to give their hearts to Jesus. Although the student newspaper was positive about what two friends and I had done, it was an embarrassment to my family. "Religion" was not something you talked about in public.

Then Mom did something I had never seen her do before and was totally out of character for her. My parents never abused me as a child. They treated me well. However, that night Mom took a belt and began beating me over the head. She beat me until I could do nothing but run out of the house. When I was in the street, she shouted, "Don't ever come back in this house again!"

As I walked down the street that lonely night, tears slowly ran down my cheeks and fell to the dry pavement. I loved my mother; I loved my family; and I did not mean to embarrass them. I just wanted my friends at LSU to know what God could do in their lives. Many were getting stoned on drugs because they had no purpose in life. I had found purpose and meaning, and I wanted them to know what I had found.

I thought that would be the worst I could go through, but it was not. A couple of years later, I met the girl with whom I would spend the rest of my life. She was a beautiful, young woman who had moved recently from Texas to Louisiana. Consequently, everyone called her "Tex.." We fell in love; and the day that I planned to propose to her, my dad became seriously ill and died.

I was with him in the hospital that day. He and Mom had finally accepted the fact that I was going into the ministry. However, they felt I should get my doctorate and become a successful pastor of a "First Baptist Church." For them, that would give a sense of respect back to our family. His last words to me that day were:

"Sammy, before I die, I have just one request. Finish your education. You can achieve so much. However, get as much education as possible. Do this for your mother and me."

I held back the tears and simply said, "Dad, I love you." I was with him when he died.

Three months later, Tex and I were married and deeply in love. We dreamed together about reaching our contemporaries for Christ. So many of our friends were wounded or killed or had lost all sense of life's purpose during the Vietnam War. While I was a senior in college, our hearts broke for them. Every time I went to class, all I could think about were my friends who needed Jesus.

I could not stay in school any longer. I had to try to reach as many of them as possible. My passion was to share God's love with those who were dying or traumatized by a seemingly senseless war. I had found peace and wanted them to know that peace. Tex was so sweet about it. "I'll go with you anywhere. I'm with you all the way," she said. "But we need to let our families know if we're going to drop out of school." That was my greatest fear. I looked down and said, "Yea, I know."

This time I expected the response. "How can you deny your father's death wish for you!" Mom exclaimed. The only thing I could do was to pray for her.

Yet there was a sense of peace that dwelt deep within our hearts. We had no doubts we did the right thing. Time has proven it was the right decision.

Over the years, God has used my mother's rejection to bond me to the people to whom I minister. As God's plan unfolded, He has sent me to the difficult areas of the world – places where Christians lose their families and sometimes their lives because they have believed in Jesus. I very seldom speak of what happened with my mom, but there is an immediate connection between them and me. They somehow know I understand what they are going through. As the years passed, I understood God was using me to pray for my mom and using my mom to work deeply in my life.

The ways of God are so amazing. He not only used my mom to prepare me to reach people in difficult situations, but He also worked slowly but surely in her heart. My mom's bitterness subsided slowly over the next several years. Ten years before she died, I received a surprise phone call from her. "Sammy," she said desperately, "I need God. I need Jesus. I need help." I prayed with Mom on the phone, and she gave her heart to Jesus. She became one of my greatest moral supporters over those final ten years. I prayed for so many years for that moment. Mom came to Christ, and God proved to be faithful.

In 1995, Dr. Gilbert Peterson, president of Lancaster Bible College, traveled with me as I led a pastor's conference and an evangelistic meeting in the Republic of Moldova, a part of the former Soviet Union. He was so impressed with the breadth and depth of our ministry in the former Communist world that he shared something with me that totally surprised me. LBC wanted to bestow an honorary doctorate on someone who had achieved in an exceptional manner in missions. They wanted to bestow it on me. I was overwhelmed.

I purchased a plane ticket for Mom to come to

Pennsylvania for that special event. With pomp and ceremony, I marched down the aisle of the auditorium of Lancaster Bible College. As I reached the first few rows of seats, I saw my dear, sweet wife who had stood by me for so many years. Next to her were her mother and father and then our daughter. Then I saw Mom. Tears were in her eyes. I received an ovation at the end of my address.

Afterwards, Mom came to me and said words I had longed to hear from her for so long. "I'm so proud of you, Son. Today you fulfilled my dreams," she said. Tears filled my eyes. I could only think of the great hymn "Great Is Thy Faithfulness." I looked into her wet eyes and said, "Thanks, Mom. I love you."

Mom was not only one of my greatest supporters during the last several years of her life. She loved going to her Sunday school class, and one of her favorite things to do was going to her church's prayer meeting. I learned many lessons of life through Mom. However, I think I learned more about prayer than anything else. When I first became a Christian, it seemed so impossible that Mom would ever give her heart to Christ. Yet I learned many great principles of praying for my family because of my relationship with Mom. It is those lessons that have become the very foundation of what I want to share with you about praying for your family.

The first and greatest lesson that God taught me was He deeply loved my family. He is a good God. I know that sounds very basic, but it is also deeply profound. Without a conviction about the goodness and love of God stamped into our hearts, we will become weary and cease praying for our families.

God loved my mother and had a plan for her. Although I never understood what had transpired in Mom's life to produce the kind of bitterness she displayed when I became a Christian, God knew. Moreover, He understood her. He loved my mom. He knew everything about her, and He knew how to gently draw her to Himself.

That is the first and greatest principle Jesus taught His disciples when He taught them to pray. When He opened the door of prayer and invited His disciples to step inside, He placed their focus on the character and attributes of God. He wanted His disciples to know the goodness and greatness of God before they ever began making requests. He taught them to pray, "Our Father in heaven." He wants you and me to know and experience Him intimately. I am convinced I would never have known God in the depths of His love without having gone through those tough times with Mom.

The first attribute of God that Jesus showed His disciples was the **Fatherhood of God.** The second was the *greatness of God*. When you begin to pray for your family, you will need to know that God is a good Father who gives good gifts to His children. (Matthew 7:11) He is perfect in His goodness. Tough things take place in family life. When bad things happen to good people, you will need stamped on your heart that the Father is good. He loves you and your family. Without that being ironclad in the deepest part of your soul, you will give up. Persistence and patience are the consequences of getting to know God in His goodness and greatness. You will need both as you pray for your family.

That was what kept me going when Mom seemed so bitter. It was easy for me to look at my circumstance and think it was hopeless. However, when I placed my eyes on our Father, who is perfect in His goodness, it gave me the inner strength to keep praying.

You also will need to know He is on His throne in heaven. Without the knowledge that He rules in the affairs of our lives, you may begin to think your situation is hopeless. However, prayer is one of the ways through which God reveals Himself in His power and sovereignty. We know in part, but He possesses all knowledge. We see in part, but He sees everything – past, present, and future. Therefore, when you pray, get to know God in His goodness and His greatness. Focus on who He is.

There is a second important truth when we pray for our families – praying with faith. Jesus connected prayer and faith in the same way God joins a man and a woman in marriage. He said, "And all things, you ask in prayer, believing, you will receive" (Matthew 21:22, NASB). Jesus told His disciples a story about a woman who persisted in her requests to an unrighteous judge. He began the story by telling them the truth of persistence but concluded by explaining the importance of faith. He closed the story by asking a question, "I tell you that He will bring about justice for them quickly. However, when the Son of Man comes, will He find faith on the earth" (Luke 18:8, NASB)? Why is faith so important when we pray for our families, and where does faith come from? Without faith, we give up. We grow weary and faint. We do not have the energy to persist. However, faith energizes us. It gives us the ability to come into His presence continually. Faith brings us back to the goodness and greatness of God. When we see Him, faith rises in our hearts.

Trust stands as the foundation for every deep and meaningful relationship. My wife and I have been married for thirty-eight years, and we have grown in our love for one another. That love has grown because as we have come to know each other more intimately, we have grown in our trust for each other. As much as I love and trust my wife, there have been times when she has failed me; and there have been many more times when I have failed her. Yet as we have gotten to know each other, our trust has grown as our love has grown for one another. Then how much more is that true with God? He has never failed us. The more you know Him intimately, the more you will trust Him.

The Apostle Paul once told a jailer, ". . . Believe in the Lord Jesus, and you will be saved, you and your household" (Acts 16:31, NASB). He told the man his salvation would come to him if he had faith. Yet he did not stop there. He also told him his household (family) would be saved when he believed. Paul tied the faith of the jailer directly to the salvation of his family.

This principle of faith may be one that is very difficult for us to understand, and we may never fully understand it. What role does faith play in the salvation of our families, and how much of their salvation depends upon God's sovereign grace? That is an impossible question to answer. All I know is that our salvation is 100 percent God's doing. God saved us by His grace and His grace alone. I cannot force a person to become a Christian – even through my prayers. Nevertheless, a part of the great mystery of prayer is that God allows us to somehow participate in our loved ones coming to Christ by faithful praying. I do not understand it. I just know it works. Prayer is a part of His great plan and His wonderful mystery. It is the meeting place – where the *Sovereignty of God* and the *Will of Man* intersect. It is the place where faith rises and moves mountains that have stood in the hearts of our families for generations.

There is a third principle that helps us as we embark on praying for our families – patience and persistence. We live in a generation that demands instant gratification. However, we must learn to wait upon the Lord. ***We learn to wait upon Him in two ways. First, we wait upon Him over a long period.*** We wait with a deep- seated belief that He will answer our prayers. My grandmother never saw the answer to her prayers. When I think of her on her deathbed, she should have been despondent. From what I have read, she died believing but not having seen the answer to her prayers. She prayed without having seen but having believed.

I prayed for more than twenty years for my mom before I ever saw an answer come. Some of the greatest victories you will see in prayer will come as we learn to wait upon God for the answer. The Psalmist continually said in the Scriptures, "Wait upon the Lord."

Prayer was prominent in the life of Jesus. He taught the disciples many truths about prayer. One of the most important was persisting in prayer. When He told the story about the woman who had faith enough to persist in her requests to the judge, Jesus was not comparing the unrighteous judge to God. He was contrasting the two. If an unrighteous judge grants our requests because of persistence, then how much more will the righteous Judge of all people grant our requests? He is good, loving, and gracious. He hears, and He will respond. The purpose of our persistence is not to get Him to do something He knows will be bad for us. The purpose of persistence is it brings us repeatedly into His presence.

Then why do we need to go into His presence persistently? It is more for us than it is anything else. I can honestly say going into the presence of God for so many years of praying for my mom was the best thing that could have ever happened to me. God had more to do in me than He did in my mom. We wonder why the answer does not come immediately. Perhaps it is because God longs to have fellowship with us and mold us into His image. Waiting upon Him is an act of dependence upon Him. As I look back on the time of praying for my mom, I realize God used that to build a sense of dependence upon Him that was extremely healthy.

There is a second way in which we learn to wait upon God – by coming into His presence and waiting before Him. He longs for His children to come into His presence. As we come into His presence, we persistently bring our requests to Him. Moreover, in one Divine moment, He works wonders. Our prayers are answered – but in His time. At the same time, He changes our lives because we have spent time in His presence.

Prayer is the greatest adventure upon which man

can embark. Prayer opens hearts. It throws doors open wide. It brings you to places you would never have dreamed and arranges circumstances that would be impossible to produce by yourself. When you learn to wait in His presence, He works in unfathomable ways. That is why the Psalmist said, "My soul, wait in silence for God only, for my hope is from Him" (Psalm 62:5, NASB).

The final principle that God taught me as I learned to pray for my family was to pray with a humble, repentant heart. I was praying for Mom's repentance, but the greatest need was deep repentance in my heart. When I look back upon those years of praying for my mom, I can clearly identify a moment when things began to change in her. She began to change when I began to change.

One day when I was having a time alone with God, the Holy Spirit opened the hidden parts of my heart and began to search them. One of the things God made known during those moments was an attitude I had not been willing to face. I had been an ungrateful son. I had never expressed to my parents my love and appreciation for all they had done for me. Selfishness was the root cause of that attitude. I never saw what their needs were because I was so wrapped up in my problems and myself.

When God opened my eyes to see my sins, I was broken. God promised that a broken heart and contrite spirit He would not despise. (Psalm 51:17) I knew I needed to call Mom, apologize to her, and ask her forgiveness. However, because of all that had occurred previously, I did not know what to expect. After mustering some courage, I called Mom and told her what God had shown me. Her response, once again, took me by surprise.

"Son," she said, "I can't tell you how much that means. Thank you so much."

Wow! Everything changed in my relationship with Mom from that moment on. It did not mean she gave her life to Christ immediately. However, it did mean she was much more open to hearing what God was doing in my life. It was a defining moment in our relationship, and it seemed to allow the Holy Spirit to begin to tenderize her heart.

I do not think that phone call would have ever come when she said, "Sammy, I need God. I need Jesus. I need a church. I need help." However, after twenty years of praying, that incredible moment came. My brokenness softened the soil of my mom's heart. My repentance made the ground fertile.

The greatest encouragement I can offer to you about praying for your family is to ask God to search your heart and show you anything that needs removing from your life. The release of God's Spirit upon their lives begins in your heart and soul. Find a time and place to meet with God. Get to know Him as "our Father." See how mighty He is in heaven. As you develop an intimate relationship with Him, faith will rise in your heart and patience will rest on your soul. God will change you more than God will change the person for whom you are praying. Wait upon the Lord.

PRAYING FOR YOUR FAMILY

1. Write down your initial thoughts about this chapter.

2. How do your family members react to the concept of receiving Christ as Savior? Are they negative or positive towards Christianity in general?

_____ Negative

_____ Positive

_____ Indifferent

3. Sometimes all we can do for the loved ones who reject our faith is to pray for them. Is it easy or difficult to pray for your family? Why?

4. Jesus said, "All things, you ask in prayer, believing, you will receive (Matthew 21:22). You must trust that God hears and answers you. Read Hebrews 11:1-12. What evidence do you have, in fact, that God does answer the prayers of His people?

Did those saints of old receive what they wanted right away?

Why do you suppose God sometimes delays His answers to your prayers?

5. Read Psalms 40:1-11 and personalize it—make it your own prayer to God. Commit yourself to being patient and persistent in your prayers for your family.

Chapter Three

Praying for Your Children

"Your kingdom come, your will be done, on earth, as it is in heaven."
[Matthew 6:10, NASB]

Billy Hobbs had everything a young man could desire and everything he had ever dreamed. An All-America football star at Texas A&M and the Most Valuable Player in the Cotton Bowl, he was under contract to play for the Philadelphia Eagles. Billy was flying high. After pulling into his home in West Texas in his brand-new sports car, he walked into his mom's home with an arrogant swagger and said to her, "I reject you, and I reject your God." His mom did not blink. She just looked at Billy and said, "I'm praying for you, Son."

More than thirty years later, Billy Hobbs was on a football field – in a different country, with a different attitude. This time he was speaking to professional football players in Sao Paulo, Brazil. "Each one of you has a decision to make," he exhorted the team. "You will choose to follow Jesus, or you will choose to live for yourself. Choose this day who you will serve." Many of the players gave their hearts to Christ, and they made Billy an honorary member of the team.

What happened to change the life of Billy Hobbs?

His mother prayed.

The most rewarding task you will ever undertake is praying for your children. It also could be the most daunting. Every time you pray for your children, it is as though you are planting the seeds of beautiful flowers deep within their souls. It takes time and care for those seeds to take root and grow. However, when they are fully mature, they bring great pleasure to the one who planted them.

Nevertheless, storms blow across their lives and threaten to destroy everything planted within them. When we pray, God provides a shelter to protect the seeds. They only produce deeper roots for the flowers to grow, and they become even more beautiful.

As I have planted seeds of prayer in the lives of my children, I have learned that praying for them does not stop once they are grown and have become independent. A parent's responsibility of prayer never ends. Our children go through various seasons of life, and God wants us to learn how to pray for them during the different seasons. You embark upon a lifelong journey when you begin praying for your children.

Before you set out on the journey of praying for your children, one great truth must be burned into your soul. Praying for your children is not a substitute for loving your children the way God intends. When you rear your children the way God desires, there will be great power when you pray for them. Without Christ-like child rearing, a spiritual barrier hinders our attempts to pray for them. The Apostle Peter wrote about the importance of Christian living and its relationship to our prayer lives. He said disobedient husbands could be won without a word spoken to them because of the godly behavior of wives. He also said the way a man treats his wife could hinder his prayers. (1 Peter 3:1-7) The way we live is the engine that enables our families' lives to be changed, and prayer is the fuel that gives the engine power and force.

There are some wonderful principles I have learned on this journey of praying for our children. At the same time, I want to be very clear in stating that our children are not perfect. They have not become super saints just because we have prayed for them. Super saints – they are not. Sinners saved by grace – they are. It does not mean there were neither pain nor problems just because we have prayed for our children. They still went through the process of trying to discover themselves as teenagers. They tested our limits at times. They had to find their faith when they went away to college. However, prayer has guided them through those tumultuous times.

My wife and I have prayed for more than three decades for our children. God taught us some wonderful principles of prayer during those years. I believe they will be very helpful to you as you pray for your children. Different people will apply these principles in different ways. Some readers may be new to the journey of prayer, and their children are already grown. Others may be brand-new parents. Each of us will want to apply the principles that are relevant to our situation.

The first principle is *surrendering our children to God.* There is a tremendous story in the Bible of a woman who wanted to have a child, but it seemed impossible. She wept bitterly before the Lord, asking Him to give her a son. Finally, she said, " 'O LORD of hosts, if You will indeed look on the affliction of Your maidservant and remember me, and not forget Your maidservant, but will give Your maidservant a son, then I will give him to the LORD all the days of his life, and a razor shall never come on his head" (1 Samuel 1:11, NASB). God gave her a son; and she kept her vow to the Lord, saying, " 'For this boy I prayed, and the LORD has given me my petition which I asked of Him. So I have also dedicated him to the LORD; as long as he lives he is dedicated to the LORD.' And he worshiped the LORD there." (1 Samuel 1:27-28, NASB).

Hannah recognized that children are a gift from God. When God answered her prayer and gave her a child, she, in turn, gave the child back to God. She understood a very simple but important truth. All life comes from God. He gives life, sustains life, and takes life. He is the only true Source of life. It is the first truth we must learn about our children. That truth produces a certain security within them and within our hearts. When Hannah came to grips with this great truth, she gave her son back to God.

My wife and I gave both of our children to the Lord before they were ever born. While they were still in their mother's womb, we dedicated them to God. Even before conception, we prayed for them. When my wife and I were married, we went to Gulf Shores, Alabama for our honeymoon. We gave each other a Bible for a wedding present. We read that Bible on our honeymoon and prayed. We dedicated our lives and marriage to God. We also dedicated any children that God would give us to Him.

When we learned my wife Tex was pregnant with our son Dave, we laid hands on her womb, prayed, and dedicated him to Christ. We did the same thing with our daughter Renee before she was born. God wants us to fill this planet with children who love God and will serve Him.

That was His plan in the beginning with Adam and Eve when He told them, "Be fruitful and multiply, and fill the earth, and subdue it. . ." (Genesis 1:28, NASB). He gave that commission before their fall. At that time, they were living in an intimate relationship with God; and He wanted that relationship reproduced around the world. He desired that the world be filled with people who loved Him.

He longs to work in our children to fill the earth with people who walk intimately with Him. Since we dedicated our children to God, I have been convinced there has been an unseen Hand guiding them. When they have made a wrong turn in life, His Hand led them gently back to the path of life. When trouble knocked at their door, the Hand of God opened it and trouble had to flee. I watched the sovereignty of God – coupled with the decision we made to dedicate our children to God – form a circle of protection around them.

Perhaps some readers might feel discouraged because they did not dedicate their children to God before they were born. That is the wonderful thing about God's grace. You can do it right now. Now is the acceptable time. Today is the day. The best time to dedicate your children is at this moment. When I speak about dedicating your children to God, I am not necessarily speaking of a ceremony in a church service. You can do that as well. However, you can give them to God in your secret place of prayer – at your meeting place. I would encourage you to dedicate your children to the Lord – no matter how old they are. Perhaps you did not know Christ or did not know how to pray for your children when they were born. God knows and He understands. Remember He loves you and your family. Allow this study to be the starting point for dedicating your children to God.

God may have blessed you with adopted children. This principle applies to them as well. God has given you a deep love for them and the responsibility to care for them. With this responsibility comes an equal measure of spiritual authority. Dedicate them to Christ in your secret place of prayer. It is no accident you chose to adopt them. The sovereignty of God and your choice have landed you in a wonderful place that enables you to intercede for them. God must have a special plan for their lives. He placed those children in your heart and now in your home.

It lies within our spiritual authority to pray for our grandchildren in a similar manner. God has told us He is faithful to a thousand generations of those who love Him. In Deuteronomy, God told the children of Israel, "Know therefore that the LORD your God, He is God, the faithful God, who keeps His covenant and His loving kindness to a thousandth generation with those who love

Him and keep His commandments" (Deuteronomy 7:9, NASB).

I cannot prove it, but I have an educated guess that my fourth great grandparents committed their future descendants to God. The reason I call it a guess is because I do not have any concrete documentation of the prayers of my grandparents several generations back. However, when I see the fruit of their lives for several generations, my guess becomes concrete evidence that they prayed for future generations. As we shall see in chapter four, my third-great grandmother humbled herself before a church that she was instrumental in forming and sought forgiveness from its members. For generations to come, the children, grandchildren, and great-grandchildren of Delaney Bass would follow Jesus and love Him with their whole heart.

Many people have become discouraged because they have given their children and grandchildren back to God. Nevertheless, they continue to live far away from God. When that happens, we must be sure we are applying the second principle – ***claiming the promises of God for our children.*** God has promised so much in His Word. Those promises are lying there like great treasures awaiting discovery. As you go to your meeting place, bring God's Word with you. The Bible says, ". . . faith comes from hearing, and hearing by the word of Christ" (Romans 10:17, NASB).

God has given my wife and me promises for both our children. Our son Dave was born in Chicago, and our daughter Renee was born in a quaint village in the Swiss Alps. Both came at special times in our lives. God spoke to our hearts about Dave and Renee and their walk with God. We have been so blessed to see much of the fulfillment of those promises.

When I write about claiming the promises of God, many people misunderstand what that means. They begin a desperate search for a promise from the Scriptures to try to find something that says what they desire for their children. The problem with that approach is that anyone can make the Bible say just about anything he wants it to say. Out of the desperate desires of their hearts, they find something in the Bible that says what they want to hear. That is not claiming the promises of God. It is creating an illusion rather than claiming a solid promise from God.

If we apply the principle of claiming God's promises for our children, then the meeting place must play a critical role in the application of the principle. We come with one single motivation to the meeting place – to know and love God. We approach the meeting place with a heart to share with Him what is on our hearts and listen to what is on His heart. We find sweet communion with God in the secret place.

Prayer is, in its most basic form, the communion of two hearts. Out of those two hearts – the heart of God and the heart of man, to which one do you think we ought to pay the most attention? The Bible describes the heart of man as being "more deceitful than all else" and "desperately sick" (Jeremiah 17:9, NASB). Yet the heart of God is pure, holy, and trustworthy. Of those two hearts, which should we spend most of our time praying about?

Obviously, it is the heart of God. How do we get to know what is on His heart? Read His Word. We find the heart, nature, and attributes of God in the Scriptures. As we read systematically through the Bible, He speaks to us. That is why we call the Bible the Word of God. If you want to hear what He has to say, then you must go to the place where He is speaking. You do not go to math class to hear a biology lesson. If you want to hear God speak, then you need to go regularly to the place where He is talking. You do not go there with an agenda. You go there to listen. He will speak. One day a Scripture verse will leap off the page, and you will know He has spoken. He will speak about the things that are so close to your heart. He will speak to you about your children.

When your children walk away from God, you can rest assured He will fulfill His promise. Everything may appear bleak on the outside, but God will fill your heart with a peace that passes all understanding. Many years ago, God gave us a promise for our son Dave. That promise came from systematically reading the Bible. We were not looking for it. Yet, in my quiet place and time alone with Him, a passage jumped off the page and landed in my heart. The promise said God would use him for His glory and he would fulfill much of the vision that God had given me.

My wife and I did not share that promise with him while he was growing up. We simply tucked it away in our hearts and would occasionally remind God of His promise. However, Dave had big plans that seemed contrary to the promise that God had given to us. He planned to make a lot of money. While in high school, he told us he wanted to go into business and make money to support our ministry. We told him our only desire was for him to discover God's plan for his life and diligently follow that plan. However, I had a promise that said something completely different from what Dave desired. I did not tell him about the promise because I wanted God to work in his heart and show him clearly His will. I wanted to make sure I was not manipulating circumstances. I knew my responsibility was not to be a replacement for the Holy Spirit but only to be available to the Holy Spirit to teach me how to pray for Dave. I simply wanted God to speak to him as clearly as He had spoken to me.

Dave walked away from God while at the university. However, God did not walk away from His promise. The only thing my wife and I had to hold on to for those years was the promise of God.

Then God intervened. Dave enrolled in a discipleship training school where the students spent six months developing their walk with God and three months overseas. While he was overseas, Tex and I received a phone call from Siberia. "Dad," Dave said, "I needed to call you and tell you what has happened. God called me into the ministry." My wife and I wept for joy. God was faithful to His promise. It is impossible to express how great the joy was to see the Holy Spirit work in Dave to fulfill the promise that God gave us when Dave was just a small child. God gave us promises for our daughter as well. It has been an incredible journey of watching God bring to pass all He said He would do in the lives of our children.

Not only have we claimed the promises of God for their lives, but also we had one great desire on our hearts. We prayed that Dave and Renee would develop a deep, abiding relationship with God. We dedicated them to God. We claimed the promises of God. Then we prayed ***they would grow in their love for the Savior.*** The longing of our hearts was that Dave and Renee would develop a deep, personal relationship with Christ and grow in their intimacy with Him. Nothing else really matters. If they really know and love Christ, all of the other things in their lives will fall into place.

Sometimes our view of the promises of God can be subjective. However, there is an objective standard that Jesus set for all of us – " 'YOU SHALL LOVE THE LORD YOUR GOD WITH ALL YOUR HEART, AND WITH ALL YOUR SOUL, AND WITH ALL YOUR MIND.' ... The second is like it, 'YOU SHALL LOVE YOUR NEIGHBOR AS YOURSELF' " (Matthew 22:37, 39, NASB). My wife and I have prayed that our children would give their lives to those two commandments. If they do those two things, they will have fulfilled life's purpose. There is something wonderful about praying those two commandments over your children. We know God will hear and answer that prayer. It is completely clear. God wants all of us to do two things in life – love Him and love people. Therefore, when we pray for those two characteristics to become the center of their lives, we can rest assured God hears us and will give us the requests we have asked. How can I be so bold to say that? He told us in His Word that "if we ask anything according to His will, He hears us" (1 John 5:14,

NASB). He went on to promise if we are sure He hears us, then we can rest assured He will grant our requests. (1 John 5:14-15)

We must remember that God has many children, but He does not have one single grandchild. Therefore, we must pray that our children develop a personal relationship with God. It must be one that stands by itself and is not dependent upon us. They need to come to grips with their relationship with Christ. My wife and I have had one passionate prayer that we have continuously lifted up to God for our children. We have prayed they would come to know and love Christ.

God will work in extraordinary ways when we pray for our children according to those things He clearly promised in His Word. I have watched in amazement and awe at how Renee has developed a love for God and for the world. She has traveled to places like Rwanda and Angola, Africa to minister to children whose parents died with the deadly AIDS virus. God has placed a deep love in her for the hurting and needy.

We watched God work this principle into Dave's life not long after terrorists attacked the Pentagon and the World Trade Center on September 11, 2001, fear gripped America. I received a double portion of it because I was scheduled to preach in a large evangelistic meeting in Khartoum, Sudan in October 2001. Osama bin Laden, the mastermind behind that attack, built the airport in Khartoum; and al-Qaeda, the Islamic militant organization of which bin Laden is the founder, was still functioning in the city. Government forces had fired upon Christians during Easter celebrations a few months earlier. After the terrorist attacks on America, I found myself in a very lonely position. People who had planned to travel with me to Khartoum were very reluctant to continue with those plans.

I went to my "*meeting place*" – the place under the trees where I meet with God regularly. I poured my heart out to God, crying, "Oh, God." I wept, "I'm willing to go alone to Khartoum, but You know that I'm a coward. Would You please send someone with me?"

After my time alone with the Lord, I went home where my wife was taking care of our granddaughter. When our son came to pick her up, he asked me, "Dad, are you still going to Sudan?" When I responded affirmatively and told him I did not have anyone to go with me, he then asked, "Can I go with you? God has placed a burden on my heart for Sudan."

Dave and a pastor from Georgia went with me to Sudan. A film crew from Brazil also traveled with us. It was an incredible experience. When I preached the first day in the stadium, nearly 5,000 people responded, saying they desired a personal relationship with Christ. My heart was thrilled and overwhelmed. I thought to myself, *If this is what happened on the first day, then what will take place the remainder of the week?*

However, there was a knock on the door the next morning. The committee of pastors and leaders at the door looked grim. "Al-Qaeda and the Muslim Brotherhood have threatened a bloodbath at the stadium if we continue. Consequently, the government has surrounded the stadium with troops, and no one can go inside. They have closed our meeting. The pastors of the city have met. We believe that you should speak to all of us. We need God to set our hearts aflame and give us courage. If we back down now, the Islamic extremists will try to destroy Christianity in our nation. We want to know if you would be willing to do that. However, there is one thing that you must know. Every Christian leader in the city will be at that meeting. If the radicals want to destroy the Christian church in Khartoum, all they have to do is throw a bomb inside the building where we are meeting, and they will kill everyone – you included. If you speak, then you must be willing to die. Therefore, you and your team pray about it and let us know what we need to do."

I cannot tell you how quickly my heart turned from excitement and elation to discouragement and deflation. Nevertheless, in the next several hours, God would answer a prayer that my wife and I had prayed for many years. I met with the small team and asked, "What do you feel you should do? I believe that God wants me to speak at this meeting with these pastors. However, no one is obligated to go to this meeting with me. You should not feel guilty if you believe that God wants you to stay at the hotel. It's a decision between you and God."

The Brazilians immediately asked, "Pastor Sammy, what are you going to do?" I told them I would speak to the leaders. Then they immediately said, "God has told us to go wherever you go. We're going also."

Pastor Greg said he was going with me. Then Dave spoke very honestly, "I need to spend some time in prayer about this." We gave him that liberty. He needed to ask God if it was His will, and he needed to come to grips with the possibility of dying for the sake of Christ. After some time in prayer, God gave him peace. He went with us. I was so blessed as I watched Dave go through the process of asking some of life's most basic questions. The Holy Spirit deepened His love for the Savior to a point that I could never have imagined. He went to the meeting.

In order for us to pray for our children to love God with all of their hearts, then we need to *pray that God will bring circumstances and people into their lives that will make an impact upon them for Christ.* This principle contains the power to redirect our children when they have gone astray as well as direct them when they are on the right path. God is sovereign. When our children make bad decisions, He has the ability to intervene at the most unusual moments of their lives.

When Dave walked down a dangerous path while in the university, my wife and I continually prayed according to this principle. There were times when God answered our prayers. Yet we were completely unaware of God's work until years later when Dave shared some of the experiences with us. He told us of one such encounter when he and some of his friends had played basketball. Afterwards, they went to a local coffee shop to hang out. A waitress took their order and then said to those four guys, "I have a question for you guys. If you were to die right now, do you have the assurance that you would go to heaven?"

When Dave told us about the waitress, I realized how much courage it must have taken for that young lady to ask four basketball players that question. Yet she obeyed God. She will probably never know until she gets to heaven that she was an answer to our prayers.

We watched God work in our son's life to bring people and circumstances into his life to direct him and redirect him. Nevertheless, God used Dave to influence our daughter Renee. She and Dave have maintained a wonderful relationship in their adult years. When Renee graduated from college, God used Dave to influence her. She began working with Dave's ministry. We have watched her grow in God's grace and mature in her faith.

There is another principle of praying for your children that has been important to my wife and me. We have learned to *pray about the things that are more important to them than to us.* Satan often places a subtle temptation in our hearts. We pray selfishly. We spend most of our time in prayer asking God about the things that are significant to us, but we spend little time praying about the things that are vital to our children.

God places many important things on our hearts about which we need to pray. However, if we are not careful, we can pray only about those things and never pray about the things that matter to our children. We can develop a selfish spirit in our prayer lives. God speaks about this in the book of James when He says, "You ask and do not receive, because you ask with wrong motives, so that you may spend it on your pleasures" (James 4:3, NASB).

There are often things that are very important to our children that may not seem as important to us. They need to know we are concerned about their interests as much as our desires. When we pray about the things that are close to their hearts, it not only releases God's power to work in those circumstances, but it also endears us to them. We will find them coming to us more often, asking if we will pray for them. It produces a very positive effect that encourages more prayer.

A "romantic" would be a great description for our daughter. When she was engaged in marriage, she wanted to have the wedding in Hawaii. Tex and I had accrued more than one million airline miles, which made that a great possibility. We had enough miles to provide tickets for both families and even some hotel rooms. Everyone was excited about going there. We found a beautiful, private location on the beach. However, there was one minor problem – rain. It rained every day we were in Hawaii.

Renee came to me saying, "Dad, you need to be praying about the rain."

I have been in situations in my evangelistic ministry where I have prayed about the rain. However, I am not Elijah. Because I preach in many outdoor settings like stadiums and open fields, we often have to deal with the problem of rain. I have never prayed for God to stop the rain. However, I have prayed that the rain would not stop the kingdom of God from coming and His will from being done. We have seen God work miraculously. However, that is another story and another book.

I did not have the same confidence to pray about the rain when it came to praying for our daughter's wedding. I rationalized our outdoor evangelistic meeting was "kingdom" business. I felt our daughter's wedding was "family" business. Therefore, I did not have the same level of faith in praying for the wedding. Nevertheless, I found a "meeting place" there in Hawaii. As I spent time alone with God, He spoke deeply to my heart. That wedding was more important to Renee than the evangelistic meetings were to me. It was one of the most important days of her life. Why then did I think God was not interested in the weather for the wedding?

I began to pray about the weather. I did not ask God to stop the rain. I just began to pray that the weather would not stop the beauty, wonder, and majesty of what would transpire that day. I prayed everyone would recognize God was the One who ordained the marriage. When we awoke that special day, there was not a cloud in the sky. It was the only day we were in Hawaii that it did not rain. After the wedding concluded, everyone marveled at "how God held back the rain." All present commented that God's blessings were certainly upon this marriage.

Renee and her husband Paul have been such a wonderful blessing to Tex and me. Immediately following the wedding, Renee gave both Tex and me a letter she had written. It is so precious that I carry that letter with me in my wallet. When I become discouraged, I take out that letter and read it. It is such an inspiration and encouragement to me. Because I prayed about that which was important to Renee, she has never forgotten it. It endeared me to her in a way that would have been impossible otherwise.

There is one final principle that I would mention – *praying for your children's spouse/future spouse.* The greatest decision that your children will ever make is the decision to give their hearts and lives to Christ. However, the second greatest decision is whom they marry. Those two decisions will make an incredible difference in the quality of their lives. We cannot make either one of those decisions for them. They have those choices to make. We cannot manipulate – and need to be very careful not to attempt to manipulate – either one of those decisions. However, we can have great influence in those decisions in our secret "meeting place."

When our children were still in Tex's womb, we began praying for the person each would marry. God has answered our prayers beyond anything we anticipated. That is not flattery; it is fact. We have watched as God provided for Dave the person who completes him. Kelly has the attributes that complement Dave in so many ways. The same is true with Paul. He possesses the strengths needed in Renee's life. When I look at Paul and Kelly, my heart is overwhelmed with emotion. I thank God for His goodness in our children's lives. God answered our prayers and gave Dave and Renee His wisdom in choosing their spouses.

Tex and I now have the challenge of praying for their marriages. Before we go to sleep every night, we pray for Dave and Kelly and for Paul and Renee. We pray for our grandchildren. We ask God to fill them with a love for the Savior and a love for one another, which is God's purpose for their lives. We have great confidence He will answer those prayers that line up with His heart's desires.

As you pray for your children, you will be amazed at God's provisions and His answers. There are two important factors to consider as you pray through these principles. First, prayer is not a magic formula to solve all of your children's problems. Those problems often cause them to become the kind of people who God desires. Pray that God will reveal Himself to them in the midst of their problems. Second, when you pray for your children, remember – God will do as much in your life as He will in their lives. As you come into His presence to seek God for them, there will be a quiet work of the Holy Spirit taking place in your life. Your children will drive you to the secret "meeting place." When you come away from that meeting, you return renewed.

Children are an incredible blessing. Yet they are an even greater challenge. As we learn to pray for them biblically, God will work in our lives in a manner we never imagined. We will walk through deep valleys and climb high mountains. Through it all, He will be glorified and His name exalted higher. We will be tempted to cease praying. However, He will work His will in ways we never dreamed possible. Some of us will see instant answers to our prayers for our children. Others will be like my grandmother. We may never understand what God has done until we go to heaven. Nevertheless, we must always remember that God will never forget the cries of His children for their children.

---

1. Write down your initial thoughts about this chapter.

2. List the names of your children and your main prayer requests for them next to their names. If you do not have children, list the names of people who are your children "in the faith"—the people who look to you to show them how to have a godly life.

3. The first principle of praying for your children is that you must surrender your children to God. This is made easier when you fully embrace the truth found in Psalms 127:3, Summarize the principle in your own words below.

4. The second principle when praying for your children is to claim the promises of God for them. This does not mean you go son a cafeteria-style search for blessings in the Bible. Rather, it means that yo hallow God to show you what to pray for on their behalf through His Word. Read 2 Peter 1:4. For what reason were we given His promises?

Is God bringing any promises to your mind as you pray?

PRAYING FOR YOUR FAMILY

5. Another principle is to pray about the things that are important to your children and not just the things that are important to you. Have you asked your children to tell you how they would want you to pray for them? Ask them, and write what they say and begin praying for them.

Chapter Four

Praying With a Forgiving Heart

"And forgive us our sins, for we ourselves also forgive everyone who is indebted to us. . . ."
[Luke 11:4, NASB]

After the phone call came from the man in Portugal, who thought he was my brother, my heart longed to know my family's history. I began searching the Internet for any clues to assist me in my quest. One of the first articles I found was on the home page of Amiable Baptist Church, one of Louisiana's first Baptist churches. It stated that John and Delaney Bass, my third-great grandparents were founding members of this historic church in Louisiana. Delaney's mother gave the land for what was probably the first Baptist church west of the Mississippi River. [1]

All of this intrigued me greatly. I phoned the church to see if I could obtain any more information. When I spoke with the church historian, she had heard me speak several years earlier at Louisiana College. When I told her my background, she asked if I would speak at the 177th anniversary celebration of the church. I was thrilled to accept the invitation.

I arrived early for the service and viewed old photos and the original minutes of the church. Two things I saw at the church gripped my heart. First, the publicity materials brought tears to my eyes. When I speak in large meetings around the world, posters, billboards, and television commercials fill the community, telling about our meetings. The local churches promote the meetings by advertising my travels and accomplishments. However, Amiable's small publicity flyer promoted my speaking in a way I had never seen. It simply read, "Hear Sammy Tippit – descendant of John Bass." My heart felt a sense of joy and warmth I had not known before. I bowed my head and softly thanked God for my ancestral grandparents, something I had never done before that day.

Yet there was one more thing I saw which put a smile on my face. As I read the handwritten minutes, penned nearly 200 hundred years earlier, great joy flooded my soul. John and Delaney were founding members of the church, and John was the first person elected to represent the church at the newly formed Louisiana Association of Baptist Churches.

As I continued going through these historical documents, I discovered some interesting procedures practiced by the church. They would not conduct any church business if there were broken relationships among the congregants. The church secretary was required to declare that the church was at peace before dealing with any business of the church. As I read the minutes, my third-great grandmother's name brought a big smile to my face. On August 21, 1830, the church was not declared at peace because Sister Bass had offended a Brother Phares and his wife. The church minutes recorded, "Sister Bass confessed her wrong and was forgiven by all the membership...." [2]

When I read about my grandmother, I immediately laughed and told my wife, "Yes. That was definitely my grandmother." I have been in more trouble in my life for saying things I ought not to have said than anything else. However, what blessed me so greatly was to see that Delaney Bass had enough humility to ask the church to forgive her. Churches today would do well to reinstate that practice before conducting formal business.

As the weekend celebrations concluded, the church secretary stood and declared, "The church is at peace." For 177 years, they had maintained their tradition of making sure everyone was at peace with each other. It is no wonder the church has remained healthy for nearly 200 years. They learned to practice forgiveness and never forgot it.

Forgiveness produces peace – in the church, in a nation, and most importantly, in the family. It sits as the centerpiece of Christian praying, and it especially rests at the heart of praying for your family. When the Bible says to "draw near with confidence to the throne of grace" (Hebrews 4:16a, NASB), it explains that bold praying is directly linked to God's forgiveness. Grace is the heart expression of one who is forgiven solely because of God's unmerited favor.

Christian praying is remarkably different from every other form of religious praying. Christian praying begins at the cross of Christ – the place where God's grace has flowed freely throughout the ages. It reaches every continent, tribe, language, and family. The cross is that which enables us to come into the presence of the Holy One of Israel. Prayer, for the follower of Christ, is not a ritual. Nor is it a religious obligation. When the believer prays, he is coming into the presence of the One who is completely pure. The only way anyone can come into the presence of such holiness is by the grace of God. You and I have done nothing to earn the privilege of coming into His presence. Jesus paid the price for our sins when He died on the cross. Our only access into God's presence is the result of what Christ did.

When God has forgiven us, we have the supernatural ability to forgive others. God placed a well of forgiveness within us. When someone injures us, we only need to go to the well and draw upon God's grace and forgiveness. Power and freedom in prayer come from a forgiven heart and from a heart that chooses to forgive. When Jesus taught the disciples to pray, He taught the principle of forgiveness. If we are going to pray effectively, then we must be forgiven and we must forgive.

Two thieves rob us from the joy of intimacy with God – *guilt and bitterness*. Guilt is a result of our doing wrong, while bitterness normally creeps into our hearts when others have wronged us. We do not need to be captured by either one of those bandits. God's throne is one of grace. He already has done everything necessary to secure our forgiveness and given us the power to forgive others. He works miracles to show us the greatness of His forgiveness. When we understand this great truth, our prayer life explodes with faith.

Because we live in a culture of anger, it is almost impossible to watch an intellectual debate about anything on any television news channels today. People seem to be so angry. What begins as a reasonable difference of opinion turns into two or three people shouting at each other. The root of this anger in today's society lies within the family. Broken relationships have become the norm of family life. Unresolved conflicts reside in many homes and most hearts. Consequently, what we see in the living rooms of our homes on television is simply a mirror of what we have experienced in the secret rooms of our hearts.

Conflicts in culture often arise because of conflict in our families. When you read the Bible's record of the beginning of human conflict, it began in the context of family life. Adam and Eve consorted in their sin. The next generation took their guilt and made it even worse. Cain killed his brother Abel. Guilt and bitterness occupied man's heart from the very beginning. It began within the family and multiplied itself into anger, hate, prejudice, and murder.

When Jesus taught His disciples to pray, He taught two principles of prayer as it relates to forgiveness. **First, we need forgiveness. Second, we must forgive others as He has forgiven us.** Guilt is the result of doing something wrong or keeping a wrong attitude, but bitterness arises because someone has wronged us. Both destroy our prayer lives.

As we learn to pray with a forgiven heart and a forgiving spirit, God will do extraordinary things. Power to pray effectively for our families begins with a forgiven heart. It begins with deep confession and unconditional repentance. God began to change my mother's heart when I repented. I had been praying for her repentance, but the real issue was my repentance.

There are two characteristics of unconditional repentance. When God looks for a repentant heart, He looks first for a heart of humility. It takes humility to admit you are wrong. There is no need to repent if we cannot see our faults and weaknesses. Without genuine humility, it becomes impossible to house unconditional repentance in our hearts. A proud heart will never have power in prayer, but a humble heart releases all of the resources of God because it touches the very heart of God. When we see God in His holiness, His Spirit drives us to our knees in confession of sin. Once we have been completely honest, broken, and repentant, we will experience that amazing grace. Oh, what joy and power lay in such praying. Pray with a holy heart. Pray with a humble heart. Then stand back and watch God work.

However, when we lack humility, we find all kinds of conditions attached to our repentance. We begin to rationalize, "I would not have done that if . . . ." Or we say, "I was wrong, but ...."

Unconditional repentance contains completely different characteristics. It says, "I was wrong – period." No rationalization. No excuses. True humility does not know any excuses.

Several years ago, my wife and I were on our way one Sunday morning to our home church. It is not often we are able to attend church because of a heavy travel schedule. We were looking forward to seeing friends and getting caught up with things at church. However, an argument arose on the way to church. Frustration rose in my spirit, and that led to anger. Consequently, I spoke to her in a harsh manner. The Holy Spirit immediately spoke to my heart about my attitude. I knew I had wronged her, and I needed to repent. However, I rationalized my behavior, thinking my position in the argument was the correct one. Yet the Holy Spirit had not spoken to me about my position. He spoke to me about my attitude and the harshness of my voice. I refused to repent. My heart filled with pride.

When we arrived at church, I put on my "Christian" smile and greeted everyone. I sang the songs; said the "amens"; and, in general, looked very spiritual. However, deep within my heart, I knew I may have impressed the people of my church; but I certainly did not impress God. He was not looking for a great smile.

He wanted a humble heart. I attempted to pray that afternoon, and it felt as though my prayers were hitting the ceiling and bouncing back. I had no freedom in prayer until I humbled myself and admitted I was wrong and asked my wife to forgive me.

I could have kept my pride and lost my ability to pray. When God looks for those He wants to bless, He searches the secret attitudes of the heart. He seeks humility among those He answers and blesses. Humility tells us we were wrong. However, deep confession agrees with God about our sins and takes the necessary steps to forsake our wrongs. Humility declares we are wrong and have no ability to repent. Humility recognizes God's sovereignty, while confession asserts we must make choices to turn from that sin. **Humility is the chief characteristic of unconditional repentance, while confession is the completion of that repentance.**

It is very important that we confess to those we have offended. If our offense is solely against God, then we need only to confess to God. If we have wronged another person, then we need to seek forgiveness from that person. Jesus told us before we bring our gift to the altar, we need to be reconciled to our brothers and sisters in Christ. (Matthew 5:23-24) Our circle of confession needs to be the same size as our circle of offense.

So many broken relationships exist within families that it has left many Christians powerless in prayer. We need to do whatever is necessary to right relationships that have been broken. This is so near to the heart of God that He sent His Son to pour His grace upon us and enable us to live in peace with those closest to us. You may be thinking it is impossible to confess to some people in your family who you have wronged. You may not even know how to find the person. God recently showed me His power in such a situation.

I grew up in Baton Rouge, Louisiana during the 1950s and 60s. African Americans enrolled at Istrouma High School for the first time. It was a historical moment. Segregation would not be seen after that year. Four very brave African-American girls came to Istrouma and began the process of breaking down racial barriers.

One incident etched a portrait on my heart in such a way I have never been able to forget the scene. This wasn't typically what happened during those days. The vast majority of students acted in a respectful manner, and for the most part, change took place peacefully. However, there was one conflict that stayed with me for decades. A crowd of students gathered around one of the African-American girls. While they screamed at her, she covered her face with her hands and wept. Although I harbored racist attitudes in my heart, I knew that was no way to treat any human being. I was a leader and knew I could stop what was taking place. However, I was a coward and remained silent while that girl suffered.

When I came to know Christ, God set me free from the racist attitudes I held in my heart as a youth. However, I tucked that scene from high school in my subconscious for many years. Yet God began bringing it to the forefront of my heart about twenty after high school graduation. I questioned God, "Why are you reminding me of this? I no longer live in Louisiana. I don't know where those girls live now, and I have no idea how to make contact with them."

The Holy Spirit impressed on my heart two ways to pray. First, I needed to be willing to ask their forgiveness. Second, I needed to ask God to allow me to meet one of them; so I could personally seek her forgiveness. The second part of His impression seemed impossible. However, I began praying many years ago that I would somehow be able to ask forgiveness of one of those girls. Occasionally, I mentioned it to my wife;

and we prayed together that God would work a miracle.

A few weeks after embarking upon this manuscript, our daughter-in-law wanted to have a CPR class for her family and our family. She found a company in California that had a representative in San Antonio who could give us the training. Therefore, both families gathered in Dave and Kelly's living room for an evening of CPR training. The African-American lady who led the session began by saying, "If you have a problem with my accent, it's because I grew up in Baton Rouge, Louisiana."

I quietly thought, *She is about my age. I wonder if she knew any of those girls. She might know where one of them lives. Maybe she could tell me how to make contact with them.* When she finished the class and began packing her materials, I asked, "What high school did you attend in Baton Rouge?"

A quizzical look came upon her face as she responded, "Istrouma High School."

I was flabbergasted. "What year did you attend there?" I continued. By then, I knew the answer. She was one of those four girls. I told her I graduated from Istrouma during the same time. I could see some fear on her face. I told her God had changed my life, and I had prayed for the past twenty years that I would be able to meet her and ask her forgiveness. It was awkward because I had prayed for that moment for so many years. Yet I did not expect the answer to come at a CPR class in my son and daughter-in-law's home in San Antonio, Texas forty years after the incident took place.

I could tell she also felt awkward. I stumbled through, saying, "Would you forgive me?" She stumbled through her response: "Yes, I forgive you." I decided I needed to send her a very transparent note about my sin and clearly ask her forgiveness. I sent her an email saying the following:

It was a pleasure to meet you Tuesday night at the CPR training. Thank you for instructing us. I learned much from your presentation. As I mentioned to you, I'm a graduate of Istrouma High School in Baton Rouge. When you stated you were from Baton Rouge, I began to wonder if you might have gone to Istrouma. When I asked you about that at the close of the meeting, I was really surprised at your answer. As I mentioned to you, I was not a Christian when I was a high school student. I gave my heart to Christ during my freshman year at LSU. God changed my life completely, and one of the greatest changes was in my racial attitudes.

But my reason for writing this letter is that I've prayed for nearly twenty years that God would allow me to meet those girls who were so courageous to integrate Istrouma High School in the 60s. I've felt a need to ask forgiveness. It was truly amazing when I saw you Tuesday night. I wasn't prepared and fumbled when I tried to apologize. The answer to my prayers came so unexpectedly.

As I told you Tuesday night, I was a leader on my campus at the time. The way you were treated was terrible. I didn't participate in what took place. But I was silent. As a leader, I should have stood up for what was right. But I didn't do that, and I am ashamed of my inaction. I am asking your forgiveness; and if you know how I might contact any of the others, I would like to ask their forgiveness.

It's good to see what has happened in your life since those days. God bless you.

Sincerely, Sammy Tippit

Her response was so refreshing. It was like a cool drink of water on a blistering, hot day:

Thank you. I had a great time and am glad to hear that you all got something out of the course. Your apology is most humbling and God's divine providence most remarkable. I always remembered those days but not with bitterness but a sense of sadness. On behalf of my colleagues, I accept your apology and, most importantly, God accepts your apology. Thank you for being a true leader and speaking up now. The sadness I felt turned to joy, knowing that throughout the world there are people just like you, lovers of God, making things right and making the world make sense.

What joy filled my heart when I received her response. The Holy Spirit cleansed my conscience, and awe flooded my soul because of the faithfulness of God. I realized He longed to restore relationships so much more than I did. When I thought of how He orchestrated my contact with the lady who attended my high school, I could weep only tears of joy. He brought to pass what seemed impossible. More than forty years after the incident, in a city in a different state, and through a CPR class whose offices were on the other side of the nation, God brought that lady into my son's home so that I could confess my sin and ask her forgiveness. Hallelujah! What an awesome Savior we have.

Two very important things transpired through that email correspondence. First, I received forgiveness. Second, she was able to forgive. Both sides of forgiveness are critically important to our spiritual health. We need the forgiveness of God and the forgiveness of others. Additionally, we also need to forgive. That lady lived with a healthy heart because she refused to harbor bitterness. She lived with dignity – although others treated her with indignity. She walked in grace because she traveled the road of humility. She reflected the life and spirit of Christ because she understood forgiveness. Forgiveness is at the heart of the Gospel.

I have met so many bitter people because of the hurt inflicted on them through their families. The family stands as the first and most basic human institution. God molds our personalities through the family unit. Family relationships meet our deep needs of love and acceptance. That is why it hurts so much when someone in our family disappoints us or does something to hurt us. It is so much easier to deal with pain that results from a stranger than to deal with hurt brought upon us by family members.

However, all of us experience that kind of sorrow at some time or another. It exists in the best of families. The health of a family lies within the hearts of moms, dads, brothers, sisters, and children. We build healthy hearts and stable homes when we learn to draw forgiveness from the well of God's grace. It does not matter who you are or how great a heritage you possess, you will always need God's grace to enable you to forgive those you love. Above all else, Christians are a people of grace. God saves us by His grace, keeps us by His grace, and enables us to walk daily in His grace. Because of His wonderful grace, we possess the ability to forgive those who have hurt us.

God has blessed my wife and me beyond measure. We thank Him daily for His goodness to us and our family. However, we would not be where we are today if it were not for the grace of God applied to our hearts, enabling us to forgive one another. There normally comes a crisis of grace in every family – a time where we have failed one another.

Such a crisis arose in our home after my wife and I had been married for ten years. The Hahn Baptist Church in Germany called me to be their pastor. The congregation consisted mostly of American military personnel serving in Germany. We watched God work in a wonderful manner during the first year. Even though the church was growing, Tex and I had ceased growing in our relationship with each other. When I returned home from the office one day, Tex had tears in her eyes. When I asked her what was wrong, she said, "We need to talk."

Those four words set us on a path that would determine the nature and quality of our marriage for years to come. That night she shared with me that, during her time alone with God, He spoke to her about bitterness she harbored in her heart towards me. She knew she would never be the woman God intended until she dealt with the bitterness. She told me, "I need to ask your forgiveness. There were things you did and said early in our marriage that I tucked away in my heart. That became the soil for bitterness. I quit communicating with you because you always seemed to be right, and I was always wrong."

Her words stung. God had prepared me to hear what she had to say. I told her I forgave her; but in that moment, God opened my eyes to see my arrogance and pride. He broke me. My heart melted, and I began to weep. God broke me so deeply that I felt I would never be able to preach again. I asked the leaders of our church if my wife and I could take some time off to be with each other and with God. The church was very gracious and understanding.

When Tex and I got away, we communicated more honestly than we had in years. I confessed. She confessed. We both forgave. We drew from the well of grace that God placed within us and pulled up a whole load of forgiveness. I look back on that week as the most important week in our marriage. That week we learned to forgive and be forgiven. We have failed each other many times since that week. However, we learned to appropriate the grace of God and forgive one another.

Many people wonder how it could be possible to appropriate such forgiveness. I have heard many say, "But, Sammy, you don't know what my husband/wife did to me. You do not understand how my parents treated me. You have never had your children treat you the way mine have treated me." I may have never gone through the problems you have gone through. Yet I know one thing – God's grace is sufficient.

One great truth enabled me to forgive. My sin put Jesus on the cross. Jesus did not die because of what the Jewish people or Romans did to Him. He could have called 10,000 angels to take Him off the cross. He did not do what He had the power and right to do. Only one reason existed for His death. He loved you and me so much that He took the punishment for our sins. It was your sins – my sins – that nailed Jesus to the cross. If you have not understood clearly enough what I am saying, then let me say it as plainly as possible. You and I murdered the holy Son of God.

The love of God is so great. He loved us – even though we murdered His only begotten Son. He forgave us and then placed that forgiveness deep within our hearts. No one has ever hurt me as deeply as I hurt the Father. Yet He forgave. That forgiveness lies deep within the soul of everyone whoever drinks from His well of grace. When someone hurts us, we only need to go deep into the well and pull up His grace and forgiveness. He gives us His power to forgive.

When we appropriate His forgiveness in prayer, it serves as a healing ointment for our wounded hearts. He applies His grace, and the wounds begin to heal. The scars of sorrow disappear. Our hearts become healthy. That is why Jesus taught His disciples to pray, "And forgive us our debts, as we also have forgiven our debtors" (Matthew 6:12, NASB). That principle of prayer stands as the cornerstone of your relationship with your family. Build on it, and no storm will be able to destroy your home.

---

1. Write your initial thoughts after reading this chapter.

2. How much of your family history is characterized by conflict? By peace?

Is there anything for which you need to forgive your family members?

3. Ask God to prepare your heart to forgive those members.

4. Our prayers begin at the cross—where the greatest battle for forgiveness was won. Write down the wonderful promise of 1 John 1:9.

5. There are two things that keep us from embracing God's forgiveness: guilt and bitterness. Read the following verses and note what they say.

About guilt—Psalms 32:3, 4:

About bitterness—Hebrews 12:14, 15:

6. Is there a broken relationship you need God's help to reconcile?

_____ Yes _____ No

7. Are you willing to do anything to mend those broken relationships?

_____ Yes _____ No

8. Do not allow the conflict to hinder your relationship with God. Write a prayer asking God to lead you in seeking that person's (or those persons') forgiveness.

9. How does Christ forgiveness help you to forgive others.

10. Draw from God's grace in your heart and ask God to enable you to forgive those who have hurt you. Then, pray this prayer by putting in the name of the person in the blank space. "God, I forgive _____ by the grace you have placed within my heart."

Chapter Five

Tearing Down Strongholds

"For our struggle is not against flesh and blood, but against the rulers, against the powers, against the world forces of this darkness, against the spiritual forces of wickedness in the heavenly places."
[Ephesians 6:12, NASB]

Thus far, God has blessed my wife and me with two beautiful granddaughters and a precious grandson. Dave and Kelly named both of the girls after great pioneers of the Christian faith – Hudson Taylor and Amy Carmichael. My wife and I were babysitting Taylor Renee and Riley Carmichael when the youngest put us in stitches. We roared with laughter as we watched my personality and the personality of my son emerge that evening.

Riley was a two-and-a-half-year-old, strong-willed child – just like her father and grandfather. She wanted to watch some of the children's cartoons we had on DVD. As I put a DVD in the player and turned on the television, Riley sat in her special, little chair with a seatbelt and began trying to buckle up. She struggled with it for several minutes, and the cartoon began. Like a good granddad, I offered to help. She looked at me sternly saying,

"No." She meant it, and I knew it. Therefore, I quickly backed off. Finally, after five minutes of frustration, she buckled herself in the chair. However, her contentment did not last long. She soon wanted to unbuckle the seat belt and walk around. After several minutes of aggravation, she became exasperated. I once again offered to help, and she looked at me as if to say, "Don't you dare. This is my seat belt, and I can take care of myself."

"Okay, okay." I smiled as I backed off.

She worked and worked – all to no avail. "Riley, let Gran Gran (the name my grandchildren have given to me) help you." Riley retorted quickly, "No, Gran Gran."

I backed away again. Finally, she gave up. She then stood up. Of course, she was unable to stand up straight because she had a small chair attached to her bottom. Her body was parallel to the ground, and the chair was sticking straight up in the air. She then attempted to walk. She made it about seven feet before she fell to the ground. Like a good grandfather, I rushed over to help her. What did I get for my great efforts?

Riley Carmichael Tippit swatted me away, saying, "No, Gran Gran."

My wife and I watched her lying face down on the floor with a small chair attached to her bottom, rising high in the air. We were breaking up with laughter. We could not believe her stubbornness. She would surely give up soon. She had to. Wrong.

Riley looked around and finally figured out a way to get up and sit in the chair. She did it successfully, but there was only one problem. She was turned away from the television set. Again, I tried to come to the rescue. "Okay," I said. "I'll turn you around."

"No, Gran Gran."

There she sat – with her back to the television set. No problem for Riley. She simply turned her head to watch the cartoons. I could not believe it.

Finally, she became exhausted and cried, "Gran Gran, help. Help, Gran Gran!" I quickly turned her around and unbuckled her from her chair. I was finally the hero. It would not have been so funny except I saw her dad (our son) in her when he was a small child. He was the most stubborn kid ever to grace the planet. Well, maybe. There is always the exception of his father. Stubbornness seems to be the number-one personality trait passed down in our family. Have you ever noticed that personality traits, like stubbornness, do not have to be taught to the next generation? They just seem to be in their DNA. They are just that way – the same way as their forefathers.

Personality traits are neutral. If they come under the control of God's Spirit, they become incredibly wonderful character qualities. A strong will – under the influence of the "flesh" – is stubbornness. However, when that same will comes under the control of the Holy Spirit, it becomes resoluteness. Yet, outside of God's control, they keep us from becoming the kind of people God created us. We often hear, "He's just like his father," or "she is exactly like her mother." That could be good, or it could indicate a deep need in the life of the person. Over time, some of those negative characteristics can become spiritual strongholds.

The Bible speaks of such strongholds in a Christian's life when Paul wrote to the church in Corinth saying, "For though we walk in the flesh, we do not war according to the flesh, for the weapons of our warfare are not of the flesh, but divinely powerful for the destruction of fortresses. We are destroying speculations and every lofty thing raised up against the knowledge of God, and we are taking every thought captive to the obedience of Christ" (2 Corinthians 10:3-5, NASB).

When Paul wrote that passage, he used imagery that was familiar to his background. The Romans often needed to attack Cilician forts built by pirates. The word used for <u>fortresses</u> was the same word used for the forts constructed by the pirates when they were stealing and plundering from people. (*Vincent's Word Studies in the New Testament*, 2 Corinthians 10:3-5) A spiritual stronghold is a pattern of thought, emotion, or action that enables the great thief "Satan" to rob, steal, and plunder our lives. It keeps us from an intimate knowledge of God and prevents us from doing His will. When we see such a pattern in our lives or the lives of our families, we must realize we are in a spiritual battle. We must learn then to pray accordingly.

We often allow strongholds built in three areas of our lives. When we dwell on wrong thoughts for an extended time, mental strongholds build up. When we consistently practice wrong behavior, then bad habits grow into spiritual strongholds. When we harbor unhealthy feelings, they form emotional strongholds. Whether we allow unhealthy emotions, bad habits, or bad thoughts to become strongholds, the result is the same. They rob us from an intimate relationship with God.

Many years ago, I met a young couple who loved the Lord and loved each other. They desired to serve God and do His will. Yet the young woman unexpectedly left her husband and began living an immoral lifestyle. Her behavior was completely out of character, and no one understood why it happened. She stopped going to church and lost all interest in spiritual things.

I attempted to speak with her for several weeks – all to no avail. After a few months, she finally agreed to sit down and talk with me. When I began to probe her thoughts and feelings, I discovered that a relative deeply wounded her as a child. The relative sexually abused her when she was just a small girl. When she told her parents, they refused to believe her. She felt dirty and rejected.

When she met her husband, she found a man who loved her for who she was and not for what he could get out of her. After they were married, they attempted to make God the center of their marriage. However, one day he did something that caused her to feel rejected. The emotion of rejection she harbored for so many years suddenly erupted. Satan rushed into that stronghold and robbed her of the blessing of marriage and the joy of her salvation. Thankfully, we were able to pray with her; and by God's power, she tore down Satan's fortress in her life. She and her husband were reconciled; and since then, they have maintained a healthy marriage.

Strongholds do not affect only husband/wife relationships but also parent/child relationships. As we rear our children, we often see strongholds in their lives.

In fact, it is normally much easier to spot the fortress that the spiritual "pirates" have built in their hearts than it is to recognize the strongholds in our lives. God gives us a responsibility to pray for our children when we become aware of strongholds in them. However, we have an even greater responsibility to identify and tear down the strongholds in our lives. We must learn to discern when a stronghold is under construction in our hearts and minds. It often takes years for one to be built. Therefore, the stronghold gradually becomes a normal part of our everyday lives and, thus, very difficult to recognize.

If we plan to identify strongholds in our lives, then we need to know how and where they originate. ***Strongholds normally begin in one of three ways.*** First, they are inherited – passed down from parents and/or grandparents. Second, we allow the construction of strongholds when we conform to the thought patterns of the world rather than allowing our minds to be "conformed into the image of Christ." Third, we allow the building of strongholds by the choices we make.

It is easier to discern the formation of a stronghold when we understand the different seasons of life in which they are constructed. For example, it was very easy for my wife and me to recognize that our granddaughter was a strong-willed child. We saw the same characteristic early in our son's life, and we knew I had to tear down the same stronghold in my life. Therefore, we began praying for Dave early in his life that the Holy Spirit would take control of this area of his life. When Dave was a small child, we prayed for him to come to know Christ and surrender his will to the will of God. As we prayed for years, we watched God turn stubbornness into tenacity and persistency. We saw a potential stronghold become a spiritual strength in his life. We witnessed self-will turn into resoluteness.

We often see inherited strongholds in early childhood. That is the season of life when we are most capable of discerning this kind of spiritual fortress in our children's and grandchildren's lives. We must learn to pray for them and guide them to overcome those patterns established in opposition to the knowledge of God. If we never deal with the construction of those fortresses, then we will one day reap the full harvest of fortresses that the spiritual pirates have built.

I have seen the tragedy of entire nations where attitudes, thoughts, and feelings were never brought captive to the obedience of God's Word. When Yugoslavia began to split in the 1990s, I was ministering in the Serbian part of the country. I met a young man whose heart and attitudes illustrated very clearly the devastation of strongholds passed from one generation to another. I was renting a car at the airport when he asked me what I thought about the conflict between the Serbians and Croatians that was taking place. I tried to be evasive in my answer because I did not want to get involved in a political debate.

Then he shocked me when he said, "I am Serbian. I have friends who were in my wedding party who are Croatians, but I would kill them in a minute."

My face fell. I could not believe what I was hearing. "Why?" I stammered.

He began a diatribe about World War II and how

the Croatians sided with the Nazis. My face must have shown my puzzlement when I questioned him, "But you were not even born then. Why do you harbor this anger and hatred in your heart?" He then began a discourse about his grandfather and the wrongs committed by previous generations. I realized that the bitterness of his forefathers had passed from their generation to his. That bitterness became a spiritual stronghold that would produce war between two groups of people. I have seen that in other nations and cultures as well. Actually, all of us have some negative characteristics left to us by our forefathers.

I wish I could say that as I researched my heritage, I discovered only good characteristics in my parents and grandparents. None of us will ever be able to make such a declaration. Every one of us has thirty parents/grandparents if we go back to our second-great grandparents. There were undoubtedly good characteristics in each of them as well as bad ones. We inherited some of both of those characteristics which create a very complex personality in each of us.

Each of us possesses a part of our personality that comes from our great-grandfather many generations earlier. We were all born with the nature of Adam. Therefore, each of us inherited a natural bent towards things that are wrong. The longer we allow them to remain a part of our personalities, the larger the stronghold becomes in our lives. Adam passed his nature of disobedience to his son Cain. The fruit of that fortress resulted in Cain killing his brother Abel. As humanity spread throughout the world, the fruit of Adam's sin spread just as rapidly. We can easily see that fruit in our lives and the lives of our children. That is the reason we must pray for them to come to Christ. He is the Strong One with the ability to tear down the strongholds established in our hearts.

We can clearly see inherited strongholds in our children between birth and preadolescence. Spiritual pirates build strongholds in our character by passing flaws from our forefathers to us. However, there is *a second place where we allow strongholds – the world.* We live in a world system whose philosophy stands contrary to the Word of God. The Bible tells us, "And do not be conformed to this world, but be transformed by the renewing of your mind . . ." (Romans 12:2a, NASB).

We are most susceptible to this kind of fortress being built in our lives during the teen years. During childhood, family is the most important entity in our lives. However, friends begin to replace the importance of family during the teen years. That is an extremely difficult time for young people. One of the reasons it is so difficult is that it is a transition season. Young people begin to discover what they really believe during those years. Peers often pressure them to conform to standards that are contrary to biblical principles.

When our children went away to the university, we watched them try to discover their faith. We had taught them biblical truth as they were growing up. However, they went through a time of being enticed by the "world's" way of thinking. It was a delicate season of life for them. My wife and I watched them attempt to find their way during this critical season of life. We knew prayer was not an option; it was an absolute necessity. They strayed, but I am convinced God used our prayers to bring them back to safe shores.

When Paul told believers not to be conformed to the world, the Greek word for <u>world</u> was *aion.* According to *Vine's Expository Dictionary of New Testament Words*, its literal meaning is the word <u>age.</u> In other words, we are not to be conformed to the thought patterns of the "age." Every period of history produces a new system of thought, some new idea. Yet the thought of every "age" always conflicts with God's principles of life. The natural inclination of youth is to taste the "new fruit" that their parents know have the same "old root" of thought – one that is contrary to biblical thinking. That is why Paul told the church at Corinth to take "every thought captive to the obedience of Christ" (2 Corinthians 10:5b, NASB). Thus, we must first make sure we have not clung to any thought process or philosophy that differs from God's Word. Then we must pray for our children and grandchildren as they are confronted by the philosophy of the "age." My wife and I have prayed that God would give wisdom and insight to our children to discern right from wrong and truth from lies.

There is a final manner in which we allow Satan to build strongholds in our lives – by our choices. Inherited strongholds are most easily seen and built during childhood, while the strongholds of the "age" are normally built during youth. However, Satan builds strongholds in our lives most often by the decisions we make. Most fortresses are built over a long period. They are constructed day by day, week by week, and year by year. We make daily choices that determine what kind of people we become.

Every time we make a wrong moral choice, it is as though we are permitting a pirate to put one more stone on the fortress. These strongholds are normally built during the adult years. No one has to live with the pirates. We all have choices to make. We can choose to obey the Word of God and bring captive every thought to the obedience of God's Word, or we can choose to allow the fortress to continue to build in our hearts. Every one of us travels down the road called "*Man's Will.*"

We all have important life decisions to make. Those decisions determine our effectiveness in pulling down the strongholds of which the Bible speaks. God has given us the ability to destroy any fortress that the most powerful pirate has built in our lives. He gives us weapons that "have divine power to demolish strongholds" (2 Corinthians 10:4, NIV). The first weapon is perhaps the greatest weapon you will ever utilize – prayer. People often say prayer changes things. However, prayer changes us more than it changes things. Prayer is the great work to which every Christian has been called. Oswald Chambers once wrote, "Prayer does not equip us for greater works. It is the greater work." [1]

The Bible clearly states God's eternal purpose for our lives: "For those whom He foreknew, He also predestined to become conformed to the image of His Son . . ." (Romans 8:29a, NASB). The longing of God's heart is that we become like Jesus. When the passion of our lives lines up with the passion of His heart, then we will stand back and watch God do extraordinary things.

He turns negatives into positives, wrongs into rights, and fortresses occupied by pirates into temples filled with His Spirit.

Because of the rocky relationship with my mother in the early years of my faith, I struggled with negativism. My first thoughts during the day were normally negative ones. If I had a project to complete, I initially thought of everything that could possibly go wrong. If I was scheduled to meet someone, I pondered all the reasons the person would reject me and my ideas. As I traveled to my office one morning, I realized that spiritual pirates had built a fortress in my mind. I needed to tear down that stronghold.

When I came to this realization, I began the work of tearing down that stronghold. In the meeting place where I spent time in prayer, I began daily to ask God to give me a positive spirit and attitude in life. He answered my prayers and renewed my mind and heart. Just as that fortress had been built over a long period of negative thinking, it was destroyed as I daily tore it down – brick by brick. Prayer becomes the chief weapon in the destruction of fortresses built in our minds. God enables us to bring every thought captive to the obedience of Christ.

That leads us to the second weapon of our warfare – the Holy Spirit. Prayer gives us access to God's throne where He holds all power and authority. The Holy Spirit is the part of the Trinitarian nature of God who dwells within each believer. He transports the power of heaven to our hearts to conform us into the image of Christ. The Apostle John wrote, "You are from God, little children, and have overcome them; because greater is He who is in you is than he who is in the world" (1 John 4:4, NASB).

Many years ago, a great preacher proclaimed the Gospel and a young girl gave her heart to Christ. After the worship service ended, the preacher asked the young girl, "What are you going to do when the devil knocks at the door of your heart?" The young girl paused and thought before responding, "I guess that I'll just send Jesus to the door."

She understood a great biblical truth. Our victory does not rest in our power but in the power of the One who lives within us. He is our Strength. He is our Fortress. He is the Rock of our Salvation. He is the One who enables us to overcome.

We find these first two weapons on the highway called *"The Sovereignty of God."* Prayer gives us access to the throne of God and enables us to appropriate the power and authority of Christ. The Holy Spirit dwells within us and empowers us to tear down any and every fortress that illegitimate pirates have constructed. Prayer releases the Holy Spirit to make us like Christ.

Yet God gives us a weapon we find on the highway called *"The Will of Man."* Paul, the great apostle, wrote, ". . . do not be conformed to this world, but be transformed by the renewing of your mind . . ." (Romans 12:2a, NASB). We have access to everything we need to tear down every stronghold. However, we still have a choice to make. *We must bring every thought captive to the obedience of Christ.*

William Gurnall, who lived in the mid-1600s, came under Puritan influence and penned a classic on spiritual warfare titled *Christian in Complete Armour*. He wrote, "Whether you like it or not, you must go into the ring with Satan. He has not only a general malice against the army of saints, but a particular spite against every single child of God." [2] We are in a battle. The battle belongs to the Lord. The General of generals calls the shots. He gives the orders; He holds the power. However, the soldier must fight. He has a decision to make every day – to put on his armor and do battle with the enemy or disobey the Commander in Chief.

When we choose to place our lives at God's disposal through prayer and by the power of the Holy Spirit, He renews our minds and revives our hearts. We become more like Christ. As we see victory in our lives, faith will blow across our hearts like a gentle breeze on a blistering, hot day, renewing our hearts and lives. The revived heart then will pray for those around them. Husband and wives, children and parents, brothers and sisters, and aunts and uncles will feel the impact of strongholds being torn down and fortresses being destroyed. We will begin to know that God is able to dismantle the fortresses in our lives, and that gives us faith to trust Him to do the same in the hearts of those we love so dearly. Strongholds are entrenched weaknesses. When we turn to God in prayer, we discover His strength is made perfect in our weakness (2 Corinthians 12:9) and the walls of the fortresses come tumbling down.

1. Write down your initial thoughts after reading this chapter.

2. Write out Ephesians 6:12

3. What does this verse tell you about the troubles you will face as a believer?

4. Knowing how your strongholds were formed is always helpful in tearing them down. Therefore, ask God to reveal and tear down strongholds from the following sources:

Those inherited; ones passed down from parents or grandparents. Those built as you conformed to the thought patterns of this world. Those built by poor choices.

Write down any strongholds and ask God to tear them down. Then thank God for uprooting them.

5. Write down Proverbs 16:3.

6. What important life decisions are you facing right now?

7. Read Colossians 3:1-17. Ask God to replace all your strongholds with Christ-like characteristics.

Chapter Six

Desperate Praying

"It is like the dew of Hermon coming down upon the mountains of Zion; for there the LORD commanded the blessing -- life forever."
[Psalm 133:3, NASB]

A pulpit. A young widow. The memory of a best friend. A church filled with people. All of them needed comfort, and I was there to give it to them. My legs trembled, and my heart raced. It was the third time in my fifty-seven years that I stood in this place, preaching the funeral of a best friend killed in a tragic accident. No one present could see what was happening inside of me.

Questions filled my mind, and hurt haunted my soul.

Billy Hobbs and I did friendship right. I can honestly say we were both better people because we knew each other. Billy and I had a natural bond because we were both Christian evangelists. We both had a passion to reach the world for Christ.

In many ways, we had similar backgrounds. In our younger days, Billy had achieved athletically, and I had achieved as a student leader. A two-time All-America football player for Texas A&M, he was inducted into the

A&M Football Hall of Fame. He played professional football for the Philadelphia Eagles and the New Orleans Saints.

Yet it was a few years after retiring from professional football that Billy realized he had no purpose in life. He gave his heart to Christ and passionately told others about the Savior he had come to know. My wife Tex and I developed a great friendship with Billy and his wife Kristi. God knit our hearts together one evening when Billy shared a deep burden with me. He struggled in an area of his Christian walk and did not know how to find victory. I understood exactly what he was going through. Often God has to bring high achievers through a time of deep failure to show them true victory. I had been there. I understood what it meant to be stripped of pride and self-dependency.

I told Billy about a book that helped me immensely, *The Calvary Road* by Roy Hession, a classic on spiritual renewal. I gave Billy a copy of the book, and he devoured it. He called me later and said, "Sammy, God has done a great work in my heart through reading that book. Where can I purchase more copies?" The next thing I knew, Billy was buying them by the boxes and giving them to friends. Billy and Kristi met with Tex and me every Wednesday evening we were in town. We shared and prayed together. Billy began traveling with me and assisting me in conferences. That was Billy's race. You could tell he found his race in life and ran it well. He also finished well.

Standing with me at the memorial service was my pastor, Dr. David Walker. He spoke first. He discipled

Billy when he first came to Christ. Then Coach Gene Stallings spoke. Coach Stallings talked about Billy's life on the football field. He said Billy was one of the toughest players he had ever coached. I spoke of Billy's life on the mission field – how he was one of the most Christ-like men I had ever worked with. Nearly 2,000 people packed the church. Many of Billy's former teammates were present. Through a video of his preaching three weeks earlier, Billy brought the final message at his memorial service, urging people to turn to Christ.

After the service concluded, we hosted about forty people from out of town for a meal. After the meal, friends asked me to share some of the things God was doing in our ministry. However, I began to feel weak. My body trembled, and I was unable to stand up. I became dizzy, then nauseous. I collapsed. I could not move.

Everyone became frightened, and someone called 911. Paramedics carried me out on a stretcher and rushed me to the hospital. After several hours of stabilizing my condition, the doctors sent me home. The physicians believed the emotional trauma had caused a shutdown of my system. After arriving home at 2:30 a.m., I slept for thirty out of the next thirty-two hours.

I spent the next couple of days trying to regain my strength. Then I awoke early one morning and knew I needed to go to my "meeting place." I drove to that favorite spot while the dew was still on the ground. I found a large rock upon which to sit. As I looked at the grass, a teardrop began to form in the corner of my eye. As I looked at the morning dew, my eyes caught one, single blade of grass. I wondered if the three drops of morning dew resting on it were actually my tears. Each dewdrop formed the perfect shape of a tear upon the bent and broken piece of grass. As I stared at that one blade of grass, I thought, *That grass looks just like I feel—bent and broken.*

Even though those drops of dew felt like my tears, I knew they were not mine. They were God's way of refreshing the earth. If anything, they were His "teardrops." That is when the refreshing began. I realized I stood in the need of revival in every sense of the word. My heart was bent as low as that blade of grass. Yet God understood. His teardrops would renew my heart. I then realized the dewdrops were not burdens to the grass but rather blessings. ***It was then I realized the first great truth about desperate praying. God often brings us to the place of brokenness so that we become desperate for His presence. It is then He revives our spirits and renews our hearts.***

Two thousand years earlier, Jesus made an incredible statement, "Blessed are the poor in spirit, for theirs is the kingdom of heaven. Blessed are those who mourn, for they shall be comforted" (Matthew 5:3-4, NASB). It was as though the words He spoke were like the dewdrops from heaven, falling on bent and broken listeners. As I sat, staring at that one piece of grass, Jesus' words began to fall on my bent and broken heart. Yes, I was mourning. My heart was broken. Questions that may never be answered filled my mind. I was emptied of all my strength. I was at the end of myself with nothing left to give. I was a prime target for the teardrops from heaven.

Peace began to flood my soul as I realized I was a blessed man, a happy man because Christ Himself would comfort me. His dew would renew my life. The dew comes at the end of the night to those who are bent low and broken in their hearts. His kingdom is made of such people. The thought of His comfort began to flood my mind. He makes Himself known to the hurting heart, to the broken and wounded. He refreshes us as the morning dew renews the earth.

As I meditated on the words of Jesus, strength began to fill my body. Peace covered my heart. Love began to wash over me as the waves of the sea. I realized those words contained the secret principles of success in the midst of failure, hope in the middle of despair, and courage in the face of insurmountable difficulties. The words of Jesus were words of revival to the soul. They were God's answer to the cries of the human heart.

It has been two years since that day when I saw those dewdrops at that meeting place. I realize life will never be the same. There will be no more Wednesday evenings with Billy Hobbs. We will not have the opportunity to dream and pray together. Yet I also know the presence of God in a much deeper way. I know the comfort that comes from heaven. Every time I see the dew on the morning grass, I remember it is His teardrops which comfort our hearts and renew our strength.

The world is full of broken hearts. As I have traveled to more than eighty nations, I have seen lives devastated by sickness, tragedy, and evil. Although humanity recently has experienced some of the greatest innovations known in history, broken hearts still abound.

Nations remain distressed by cataclysmic events, while terrorism has gripped the world with fear. Life, tragedy, and death – all cripple the most courageous Christians and break the bravest men and women.

Suffering is a complex subject; and there does not seem to be a concrete answer to the question, "Why do we suffer?" However, I have learned more truth and grown deeper in my faith during seasons of suffering than any other time in my life. The deepest moments of suffering for most of us come in the context of our families, the people we love the most. We hurt when they hurt. Our hearts break when something goes wrong in or with our families. Yet, during those times of pain, we often find the comfort and kingdom of God. When we become desperate, God's kingdom seems to rain down on us just like the dew refreshing the earth. His kingdom comes, and His comfort rests upon our hearts. Renewal sweeps over us.

The Psalmist said, "The sacrifices of God are a broken spirit; a broken and a contrite heart, O God, You will not despise" (Psalm 51:17, NASB). When we are broken, we pray desperately, and God does not despise the desperate prayers of wounded hearts. He makes Himself known to us in times of desperation. ***That is the second great truth I have learned. God brings us to a place of desperation because He wants to reveal Himself to us.*** I do not fully understand how or why this happens. I just know it is true that we get to know God intimately during times of suffering. Desperate praying leads us down a path called "*The Knowledge of God.*"

The nature of the kingdom of God is completely

different from any other kingdom. One word describes God's kingdom – grace. That is what distinguishes His kingdom from all other forms of government. Every culture is built upon performance. People construct entire philosophies of life on the "survival of the fittest." Nations rise or fall on military might. Religions grow or decline on duty and deeds. Economies expand and deflate on energy and effort. However, God's kingdom is a grace kingdom. Only those who are spiritually poverty-stricken can experience the kingdom of grace. Only the poor in spirit can grow in their knowledge of the King. Nothing anywhere exists like it.

"Amazing grace, how sweet the sound" is the theme song for the kingdom of God. Wonderful grace. Marvelous grace. Unmerited favor. Love abounding towards us – not because we deserve it or have done anything to obtain it. God's kingdom is all of God and nothing of ourselves.

The first drops of dew upon kingdom hearts are "grace drops." We are forgiven by grace, saved by grace. We grow in grace. The entirety of the Christian life is by grace. Our knowledge of God is completely because of the grace of God. It is interesting to note that only the bent heart can receive the grace that comes from above. Mercy and grace land on the bent and broken heart – the humble heart.

The Apostle Peter wrote, "God is opposed to the proud, but gives grace to the humble" (James 4:6b, NASB). Only the humble of heart can experience the grace of God. The proud stand tall but have no place for the dewdrops from heaven to rest. It is the lowly – the bent and broken – who have a resting place for the morning dew. It is the heart of humility where grace finds its resting place. God resides where grace rests.

There exists a third great principle I have learned about desperate praying. It is powerful praying. I found some very interesting truths about prayer when I learned about my grandmother and her special meeting place. When I first discovered my grandmother had a meeting place where she talked with God and had intimate fellowship with Him, I wondered why it was under a peach tree. I later learned something very interesting about her prayer life when I found the answer to that question. My dad had an older brother named Woodrow who died as a young child. His death crushed my grandmother. They buried him on the farm – under that peach tree.

Eliza's pain ran so deep. However, my aunt wrote about her, explaining that God met with her under that peach tree; and she had her most intimate times of talk at that meeting place. She poured out her heart to God under that tree. Her meeting place was the same place where she experienced the greatest pain in her life. She understood what it meant to pray desperately.

Eliza's desperate praying would turn into powerful praying. Those closest to her knew when Eliza cried out to God, God's will in heaven moved into human hearts on earth. My aunt Pearl Tippit Cooley chronicled the prayer life of her mother (my grandmother) and wrote, "When World War II began, another son, Tom (my father), enlisted in the service to fight for his country. Later as Mother lay dying, she prayed for Tom and again told Jesus her desire – 'Lord, I don't want my boy to die on the battlefield.'" [1] After Eliza died, Tom Tippit was in the European theater, fighting Hitler's men in a secret armored unit.

No one heard from him for a long period. When my grandfather became anxious about his son, my aunt reminded him, "They don't have enough bullets to get Tom. Mother prayed." [2] My aunt then noted, "Since that time, no son or grandson has ever been lost on a battlefield." [3]

Eliza experienced the principle of desperate praying – ***desperate praying is powerful praying.*** God hears the cries of His children.

There are two small verses in the Old Testament that give evidence that God responds mightily to desperate praying. The Bible says, "So God heard their groaning; and God remembered His covenant with Abraham, with Isaac, and Jacob. God saw the sons of Israel, and God took notice of them" (Exodus 2:24-25, NASB). God heard the cries of His children thousands of years ago and showed His compassion to them. In the following verses, God reveals Himself to Moses. Things would never be the same again in Egypt. God wrought miracles. He delivered the children of Israel with mighty signs and works. He has not changed. He still hears the cries of His people. He continues to respond to desperate praying.

When we pray with a broken heart – a desperate heart, the heart of God is moved by the hurt in our hearts. That is when the teardrops from heaven fall to the earth. That is when God sends His provision. In that moment, the Holy Spirit is released to work in ways far beyond anything we could think or imagine.

That leads us to the final and fourth principle of desperate praying. Such praying is so powerful it has the ability to revive our families, communities, and even nations. Revival falls as the dew from heaven on parched hearts here on earth. As I have traversed the globe, I have discovered something very interesting that is transpiring. God is doing extraordinary things to bring His kingdom to earth. There has never been a period in Christian history where the church has grown so rapidly. Yet much of that growth is in developing nations. Most church growth in Europe and North America is more transfer growth of church members rather than people coming to Christ. In other words, most growth of churches in the West results from people moving from one church to another one.

However, when I travel to other countries, there is tremendous growth in the church. Sometimes the greatest growth of Christians is in the most difficult places. For instance, most people are surprised to learn the fastest growing church with which I have had contact in the Middle East is in Iran. Christians have experienced great persecution there. I know people who have gone to prison for their faith in Christ. I know family members of people killed for their faith in Christ in Iran. Yet I stand amazed at the mighty work of God's Spirit inside Iran.

Much of the growth of the church in Iran comes from desperate hearts. The darkness is so great that God's people have desperately cried to Him for His light to shatter the darkness. God has answered and continues to answer their prayers. I have personally witnessed non-Christian families coming to Christ when one member of the household becomes a Christian and then cries out desperately for other family members to come to Christ. Not long thereafter, I meet or hear about their brothers and sisters, aunts and uncles, mothers and fathers coming to Christ.

It is at this point that the Sovereignty of God and the Will of Man intersect. God knows our circumstances and responds to our cries. His knowledge is rooted in His sovereignty, while our cries to Him express the deep choice we make to trust Him when our circumstances look impossible. The *Sovereignty of God* and the *Will of Man* join hands when we face difficulties in our families and cry out passionately to God. When they stand joined together at the intersection of the meeting place, they form the great mystery of prayer.

Prayer acts as a forerunner of revival. It goes ahead to prepare the way for a mighty outpouring of God's Spirit. Prayer does not force the hand of God to make Him send revival. God sends an awakening to a community when He decides. However, the great mystery of historical awakenings is that many times people have prayed; and revival did not come. Yet I know of no time in the history of the church when people ***did not*** pray and revival came. Only God holds the answer to that mystery.

The last great historical awakening descended upon the United States in 1857 when Jeremiah Lamphier began a prayer meeting in the business district of New York City. One hundred and fifty years prior to the publishing of this manuscript, a great spiritual revival began to sweep through the major cities of North America. Noon prayer meetings popped up all over Canada and the United States. Dr. Roy Fish, Distinguished Professor of Evangelism at Southwestern Baptist Theological Seminary in Texas where he has taught evangelism for forty-one years, traced the work of God in Baptist churches across the United States during that great awakening. God blessed and churches grew. Dr. Fish documented the number of baptisms in Baptist churches during the years of that mighty outpouring of God's Spirit. Churches in Wisconsin had six times more baptisms during the revival than the year preceding it; Michigan three times as many; and Ohio double the number of baptisms in their churches. [4]

That great revival did not happen by accident. A combination of the sovereignty of God and the prayers of men released God's presence across America and Canada. However, one major factor precipitated the move of God's Spirit. Dr. Fish described what transpired, "The immediate era of expansionism and prosperity had occasioned a spirit of carelessness and wildcat speculation in the nation's economy. This, coupled with financial conditions in England and on the Continent, brought about a major financial panic in October and plunged the nation into a period of severe economic depression." [5]

One cannot understand the last great revival in America until one understands that God's Spirit worked to produce a spirit of desperation in the hearts of His people to pray and seek His face. The Fulton Street prayer meeting began at the end of September of the same year of the financial collapse. A wineskin that would hold the outpouring of God's Spirit formed just days before the economic collapse in America. Proud, successful businessmen found themselves desperate and called upon the Lord. He answered. Revival swept the land.

As I observe conditions today, crisis engulfs the family. Divorce, separation, abuse, and adultery – all are common characteristics in today's homes. When we become desperate enough to cry out to God – just as they did 150 years ago, then we will create a wineskin that can contain the new wine. However, too many Christians have become professional "carpet sweepers." That is, we have learned well how to sweep our hurt and pain under the carpet. When we become desperate enough to get honest and cry to God, He will hear. He will have compassion on us. He will intervene in the affairs of our lives. He will save our families.

Desperate praying. The need of the hour. It may be the only hope for our families.

---

1. Write down your initial thoughts after reading this chapter.

2. Recall the most intense feeling of desperation that you have ever experienced. What were the circumstances surrounding that feeling?

How did that make you feel about God?

3. Write out Jeremiah 31:25.

4. How did God refresh you after that experience?

5. What does James 5:13 instruct you to do in the midst of your suffering?

6. Read 2 Corinthians 4:13-18. Personalize it—make it your prayer to God.

7. It is not your responsibility to "create" revival, but your prayers certainly precede it. Your prayers prepare your heart for the outpouring of God's Spirit. Write down 2 Chronicles 7:14.

Chapter Seven

Leaving a Legacy

"I have inherited Your testimonies forever, for they are the joy of my heart."
[Psalm 119:111, NASB]

Prayer provides you with an eternal legacy. It not only enables you to leave a lasting legacy, but prayer becomes the legacy you leave. After learning about the prayer life of my grandmother, I understood the impact she left on me, the grandson who she never met. However, I also realized her example of prayer was the inheritance she left me. Her legacy traveled three generations into the future, touching her son, grandson, and great-grandson. Prayer enabled Eliza Bass Tippit to leave a legacy longer than she could have ever imagined. She inherited a legacy from her great-grandfather and great-grandmother and then passed it to future generations she would never see.

I do not think John and Delaney Bass, the great-grandparents of Eliza Bass Tippit, had the ability to comprehend the magnitude of the decisions they made when they joined the Rev. Joseph Willis to plant some of the first Protestant churches west of the Mississippi

River. They could not have known that a third-great grandson would pioneer in evangelistic efforts in some of the most difficult places on the earth. I doubt they understood their legacy would refuse to stop.

Because I discovered John Bass was listed as a "free person of color" in the 1810 and 1820 census of St. Landry Parish in Louisiana, people have asked me if that discovery produced an identity crisis within me. Actually, it did just the opposite. It created an indescribable joy in my heart and taught me the meaning of three important words.

Heritage: something that is passed down from preceding generations, a tradition. **Identity:** the set of behavioral or personal characteristics by which an individual is recognizable as a member of a group. **Legacy:** something handed down from an ancestor or a predecessor or from the past. [1]

Heritage, identity, and legacy represent our past, present, and future. Heritage is what we have received from the past. Identity is who we are and who we become in our lifetimes. By the time we die, we have established our ultimate identity which becomes the legacy we leave for future generations.

Heritage + Identity = Legacy

We have no control over our heritage, but our heritage plus the choices we make create our identity. When the two come out of the fiery furnace of life, they produce our legacy. Heritage is a derivative of the sovereignty of God, the God who ultimately controls all of human history; while identity is the fruit of the will of man – the choices we make every single day. The sovereignty of God plus the will of man leave a legacy for future generations.

Each of us has a history – a story that joins the providence of God with the personal decisions we make daily. That history creates a personal legacy to be left with our children and grandchildren. The heritage of our families becomes the history of our nation.

What we receive from yesterday and act upon today becomes legacy tomorrow. Good or bad, we are leaving a legacy for our children and grandchildren. The fact of our legacy cannot be changed. The kind of legacy we leave is yet to be determined.

Every believer should long to leave an eternal legacy with future generations. We must learn to view life with eyes that see more than the accumulation of things. We must live with eternity in our eyes, heaven as our home, and future generations in our hearts.

We leave an eternal legacy by embracing the past, making wise decisions today, and trusting God for the future through prayer.

We begin to forge the future by learning from the past. If you long to leave an eternal legacy, then you need to go to God in prayer and thank Him for your heritage. Learn to embrace your past. When I embraced my heritage, it was as though ointment healed the wounds of my heart. When I embraced my heritage, it helped me to understand who I am and even understand why others did not understand who I am. It released me to love people in a fresh way. It freed me of emotional baggage that I needed to drop. When I was able to thank God for my heritage, I was able to understand *the first step of leaving a legacy – thanking God for creating me uniquely.*

Heritage is the suit of clothes that God gives us when we are born. He never makes two suits the same. Our personalities are an outgrowth of our heritage. Personality is neither positive nor negative. What we do with that personality is what really counts. How we use it is really what matters. However, when we learn to accept ourselves as God created us, we are on the road to becoming all He intended us to become and do all He has given us to do.

Our greatest achievements in life will come as we learn to accept the suit of clothes that God has given us and then live and work in those clothes. Embracing your heritage becomes the starting block for running the race God gave you to run. You have strengths and weaknesses. When you learn to identify those strengths and weaknesses, you have the ability to run with great success.

You may protest saying, "You don't know my forefathers. I do not possess a great heritage. My forefathers were outlaws. I don't want to be like them." Don't worry. I have some "outlaws" in my background as well. All of our forefathers had both good and bad qualities. We can choose to live by either the good or bad characteristics. When we choose God's way, we are on the road to leaving an eternal legacy.

That brings us to *the second principle that enables us to leave an eternal legacy. We must make decisions today that build us into people of high moral and spiritual character.* Personality emerges from traits handed down to us. However, character is what we do with the personality given to us. We may have the personality of our forefathers, but we do not have to develop the same kind of character they had. We can make good choices that grow us into a person of Christ-like character.

As I researched my heritage, I discovered the people in the pine forests of Louisiana – called "Redbones" – were known by the larger culture as having a bent towards violence. A couple of stories were passed down from the 1800s where the "whites" and the "Redbones" fought one another. The larger Anglo community used the term "Redbone" as a racial slur and occasionally used the "N" word to describe or address my forefathers. There was once a shootout between those called "Redbones" and the Anglos at a small place called Westport. In another incident in 1881, a riot developed because of tensions between the "whites" and the "Redbones." My grandmother would have been a young person when the 1881 riot took place.

Yet one of the greatest memories of my dad came from an experience that flies in the face of the culture in which he grew up. Dad was a big man, standing six feet and four inches tall. You would not want to mess with him. He was strong and athletic – a basketball star. He knew how to take care of himself. Yet he was not a violent man but a peaceful man.

When I was in elementary school, a basketball competitor challenged me to a fight. I refused. He and his friends began calling me "chicken." I still refused to fight. Then the other boy hit me in the face and knocked me backwards. At that moment, I remembered the words Dad taught me: "It takes a bigger man to turn the other cheek than it does to fight."

I then gathered my composure and walked within six inches of the other boy's face and turned my cheek. He hit me again, and I fell to the ground. Everyone laughed and walked away. I pulled myself off the ground and walked home by myself. It was a lonely walk. I was afraid to face my parents because I did not know what they would say when they learned what transpired.

When Dad came home, he could easily see my black eye, and he asked what happened. I told him the whole story; and I will never forget how he responded, "Son, I am so proud of you. You did the right thing."

I cannot ever remember my dad telling me he was proud of me – not even when I won athletic or academic awards. He may have said that to me, but I have forgotten it. However, I never forgot that day of the fight and Dad's response. I did not realize the complete implications of his words until I learned my heritage.

Dad must have learned to fight and defend his rights, having grown up in a community where people looked down upon his parents and grandparents because of their racial and ethnic backgrounds. Yet someone taught him the words of Jesus – that it is better to turn the other cheek than to strike a person back. I am sure that was a part of my grandfather and grandmother's spiritual DNA.

My grandparents learned to make decisions that would forge their children's futures. Their choices flew in the face of their culture.

Dad had to make the same choices. Dad made a decision not to live with a heart of bitterness, and that left me a legacy of peace because of an attitude he chose. He refused to be conformed to the culture around him. Long after Dad died, God sent me into war zones to proclaim the Prince of Peace as the hope of the nations. That has been a part of the legacy that Dad left me. He refused to live by the customs of his culture.

We do not have to live as a slave to the past. When we make the right choices, we walk down a road that leaves a Godly inheritance for future generations. Not only do we need to embrace our heritage and make Godly decisions, but we also leave an eternal legacy through our prayers. Even if our heritage is contrary to Christianity, even if we have made some very poor decisions in life, prayer has the ability to change everything. Prayer should never be an excuse for bad decisions, but prayer can transform a poor past and devastating decisions into a marvelous future. God can restore everything that Satan has destroyed. He has the ability to turn failure into victory, a feeling of rejection into a fountain of acceptance, and a dark past into a bright future.

The greatest legacy anyone can leave is that of prayer. Prayer has the ability to leap past one generation and touch the next. It can water the scorched earth of our past and pave a path for the future. Prayer has the power to change our circumstances; and when it is not in our best interest for our circumstances to change, then prayer has the ability to change us. It turns the impossible into the possible. We leave a legacy when we choose to become a people of prayer.

Several years ago, God placed me on a journey of prayer that would astonish me and change the destiny of several families. A man challenged me to pray in an unusual manner during a pastor's conference in California in 1997. He challenged me to go to Iran and pray for God to open doors for the Gospel. At that time, Iran was one of the darkest nations in the world. Radical Muslims in the country killed Christian leaders because of their faith in Christ. After some time of discussion about the matter, I decided to accept his challenge. Within a year, we were in the country. We went with only one purpose – to pray.

We walked the streets of Iran's major cities – Tehran, Shiraz, and Esfehan – and prayed. As I looked into the faces of the people, my heart broke for them. God placed a deep love in me for the Iranian people. I found them to be delightful and some of the most hospitable people in the world – much different from what I had seen on television. As we walked and prayed for ten days, I saw something that captured my heart. Satellite dishes were everywhere.

God spoke to my heart that the doors for the Gospel would open through those satellite dishes. I began praying that He would open a door to proclaim the Gospel through satellite television. When we returned to the United States, we met with Iranian Christian pastors living in southern California. We shared our burden for Iran and the vision given to us while inside Iran. I then asked the pastors, "What should I do with this burden?"

One of the pastors immediately responded, "Sammy, we need your books translated and distributed in the country." Then someone said, "Can you train our leaders?" Before the meeting concluded, my friend and I were thrust into a ministry that continues ten years later. I have had a television broadcast into Iran for the past three years. Five of my books have been translated into Farsi, the primary language of Iran; and they have been distributed throughout the nation. We have conducted leadership conferences for the past eight years. We brought leaders out of the country to a "safe place" and taught them principles of leadership. On several occasions, we taught these leaders principles of prayer. We taught them to pray that God would open doors for them to present the Gospel to people in their nation.

(The names and places in the following story are changed for security reasons.)

One church in a particular city sent leaders to our conferences every year. One day the pastor of that church was moving tiles for the church building in Iran. A man named Mohammed walked by the church as he was moving the tiles. He asked the pastor if he could help him. The pastor graciously accepted Mohammed's offer. After completing the job, the pastor gave him a New Testament as a way of saying, "Thank you."

Mohammed returned to his home and began devouring the Scriptures. His entire family could not understand what was transpiring. He was not much of a reader, but he could not put down this book. He read it morning, afternoon, and evening.

Although Mohammed was a nominal Muslim, his wife was very strong in her Islamic faith. However, they were both amazed at the teaching of the book given to him. Mohammed brought his wife, mother-in-law, and sister-in-law to the pastor; and they began attending the church. They heard the Gospel, and Mohammed came to Christ. Then his wife Mina, mother-in-law Zahra, and sister-in-law Nagmeh followed Christ. God changed the entire family. Their hearts were set aflame with the love of Christ.

Nagmeh wanted her friends to know Christ, and she began sharing God's love with them. However, that produced many difficulties. She soon determined it was no longer safe for her to stay in Iran and decided to leave there, go to the United States, and apply for political asylum. Another sister and brother-in-law lived in the States, but they were not Christians and could not believe what had taken place in the family. Yet they loved Nagmeh and wanted to help her.

After six months in the United States, Nagmeh was required to go to court for a hearing to determine whether she would be granted political asylum. Her attorney was young and inexperienced and seemed to struggle presenting her case. The judge, therefore, called Nagmeh to her desk and said, "You say you have become a Christian. Can you prove to me you are a Christian?"

That placed Nagmeh in a very difficult position. She spoke almost no English. Her court-appointed translator was a Muslim, and he did not understand many Christian terms that Nagmeh would need to use. On top of that, how would she be able to prove to an American judge that she was now a follower of Jesus?

Nagmeh looked at the judge with a sheepish expression and spoke through her translator. "No, I cannot prove to you that I am a Christian; but the Spirit of Jesus lives in me. If His Spirit lives in you, He will tell you that I am a Christian. You will know the truth."

The judge was somewhat taken aback. She then asked Nagmeh, "Would you pray?"

(Remember, all of this is taking place in an American courtroom.)

Nagmeh looked at the judge and quizzically asked, "Pray?"

"Yes," said the judge. "Pray right now."

Nagmeh bowed her head and began pouring out her heart to God with a Muslim translating her prayer to God through Christ. "Oh God," she cried. "I want Your will. I am Your child. If you want me to go back to Iran and face the persecution, then please let

Your will be done. I am willing to go back. I will do what ever You want. However, if you want me to stay here in the United States, then I pray that You would touch this judge's heart to grant me permission to stay here. In Jesus Name. Amen."

When Nagmeh opened her eyes and looked up, everyone in the courtroom was crying, including the judge. The judge immediately said, "Welcome to the United States," and she granted Nagmeh political asylum.

Her sister and brother-in-law had lived for a number of years in the United States and understood that such a scene in an American courtroom was nothing short of miraculous. God began touching their hearts. After a year, Mohammed and his wife Mina, along with their children and Mina's parents, immigrated to the United States. God answered Nagmeh's prayers for her family – with the exception of the one sister and brother-in-law.

The entire family prayed for her sister Roya and brother-in-law Amir. Nagmeh also asked friends to pray for them. Mina gave the couple a children's Bible and encouraged them to read it with their children before they went to bed at night. Roya and Amir read it the first night. However, on the second night, their nine year- old son interrupted his mother's reading and said, "Mom, Dad. God is talking to me, and He wants to say something to you right now at this moment. Look at my arms. I have goose bumps." The child then began to tell them that Jesus is the Son of God and that He is more than a prophet. He explained the concept of the Trinity to them.

Amir and Roya were astonished. They bowed their heads and placed their faith in Jesus as God's only Son. They became followers of Jesus. When I heard this story, I was completely amazed. It began with a prayer walk inside Iran, then a conference to teach pastors and leaders to pray. God changed three families and one single, young woman. Mohammed, Mina, Nagmeh, Amir, Roya, and their parents are following Jesus. They had no Christian heritage. Yet they will now leave a legacy to their children and grandchildren. Prayer has the ability to create a legacy and give it the stamp of eternity. It did with Nagmeh; it can with you. Prayer will forge your future.

My grandmother left me a legacy. However, I would have never known about it if my aunt had not written about her prayer life. The greatest blessing that my grandmother gave me was that of prayer. However, because my aunt documented her prayer life and a cousin researched our family history, I discovered the great gift left to me. It convinced me of the importance of documenting the great things God has done for us.

As I conclude this book, let me encourage you with some practical activities that will bring great joy to your life as well as to future generations. *First, research your family's spiritual lives.* It is possible you are like me. I thought I had no or very little spiritual heritage. Yet I discovered an incredible history that has given me great joy. *Second, think about the persons who have influenced you and helped you come to know Christ.* Thank God for them in prayer. Tell them how much you appreciate them. Ask them who

had an influence on their spiritual lives. Record any memories you have of your parents or grandparents praying for you. If your parents are still living, ask them the same questions and record stories of how God answered their prayers.

Third, if you are like Naqmeh and have no known Christian heritage, then it is important that you write how you came to Christ and keep a record of the answers to your prayers. Often the most amazing stories of answered prayer come from first generation

Christians. Those stories will be very important to future generations. They will learn God's plan for their lives through your experiences.

Finally, make a list of the people for whom you are praying. You may want to have two lists – one of family members and the other of people for whom you are deeply concerned. As God answers those prayers, record the circumstances and the thoughts and feelings you had when He answered your prayers. Keep a prayer diary, and give it to your children and grandchildren at a future date.

As I researched my family history, I discovered the critical importance of documents. A dull pen will always record your story more clearly than a sharp memory. Stories passed down by word of mouth have a way of changing over time. Documents will enable you to write your legacy and maintain accuracy. Most of all, it will leave no doubt that your legacy is one with eternal value.

While in the process of writing this manuscript, I traveled to South Africa to speak at a conference. When my wife and I arrived in the country, we visited the home of Perold de Beer who served on the Board of Directors of the ministry sponsoring the meetings. Perold showed me some old pictures of his family and noticed my interest in history. He pulled out a scrapbook with old newspaper articles and then said, "Somewhere in here, I have a letter written to my grandfather by Andrew Murray. My grandfather was a friend of Dr. Murray. When my grandfather had a serious accident, Andrew Murray sent him a personal, handwritten letter."

My eyes popped out! A personal, unpublished letter from Andrew Murray would be like discovering a gold mine. God used Dr. Murray 100 years ago to spark a spiritual revival in South Africa. He authored some of the greatest books ever written on the subject of prayer. Several of his books are classics.

Perold found the letter in the scrapbook. It was

written in Dutch and needed translation. Perold was gracious enough to translate it and give me permission to use it in this book. The letter spoke about the necessity of prayer and the sovereignty of God. Andrew Murray wrote a great summary for this book nearly 100 years ago. There I was, holding a document by one of the greatest authors to ever write on prayer.

Perold de Beer was greatly blessed by his grandfather because he kept that document. It found its way into the hands of his grandson two generations later and then blessed you and me. Therefore, I will close with this never published letter about prayer by Andrew Murray. By the time you finish reading it, you will know the importance of documents; but foremost, you will understand the necessity of the meeting place, the place of secret communion with God.

The following is a transcription of the original letter in Dutch from Dr. Andrew Murray. It is dated August 30, 1913 and addressed to Rev. Z. J. de Beer of Kalkabay, Cape Town, who was involved in a serious accident. The transcription is from Rev. de Beer's grandson, Rev. Perold de Beer. [2]

Dear Brother,

I received the news of the serious accident in which you were involved. So close to death, and yet, the Father did not allow it. He gave you life as a new gift. And yet, He could have protected you so easily from the accident, but would not. He wanted this new life that He gave you to be sanctified as a time of loneliness or maybe suffering, but certainly as an opportunity to know Him more closely and to have a nearer walk with Him.

We often hear the confession that we have too little time, maybe also too little desire for this secret communion with God. Christ found His strength and joy in this communion with God, and would have us also discover such strength and joy in our lives.

I pray from the depth of my heart that He would give you what you need in order to bear joyfully what He lays upon you. May He grant you a childlike commitment to learn and receive all that He lays upon you. I am sending a little booklet titled, "Eendracht maakt magt" (Unity gives power) regarding united and faithful prayer. The writer says that under the pressure of his ministry, he fell into the trap of becoming so busy that little time was left for prayer. He [God] says to you, "My servant, My son, I will see to it that you have time in abundance; you see to it, that under the guidance of My Spirit, your heart would be kept open to Me in prayer. And I will grant you the precious blessings that I planned for you in your suffering." The Lord who is mighty to bring forth light out of darkness, give you a blessed time of rest on the sick bed, as well as a blessed healing before you return to your labor.

My sincere greetings to your wife and daughter. I also include a few booklets for her.

In the love of our Lord,
Yours truly,
Andrew Murray

1. Write down your initial thoughts after reading this chapter.

2. Do you agree that, "Prayer provides you with an eternal legacy. It not only enables you to leave a lasting legacy, but prayer becomes the legacy you leave."

_____ Yes _____ No

Would you commit to being an example of prayer to future generations?

_____ Yes _____ No

3. Your personality no doubt resembles the traits handed down to you by your family. Write down the traits in yourself that remind you of your parents and grandparents.

4. Your character, on the other hand, is the result of what you allow to control your personality—whether that is the Spirit or the flesh. Read Romans 8:5-9. Are the traits you listed above under the control of the flesh or the Spirit?

_____ Flesh _____ Spirit

PRAYING FOR YOUR FAMILY

5. Write a prayer asking God to sanctify you fleshly traits and make them traits that the Spirit can use.

6. Write out Psalms 34:15.

7. You cannot control your heritage, but you can influence your identity and legacy by your daily choices. Read Psalms 37:1-7. Write down God's promises to you.

Endnotes

Introduction

1. Don Marler, *Redbones of Louisiana*, (Hemphill, Texas: Dogwood Press, 2003), 211, 218.

2. Glen Lee Greene, *House Upon a Rock*, Executive Board of the Louisiana Baptist Convention (1973), 53. (This book traces Joseph Willis, son of an Indian slave in beginning the historic Calvary Baptist Church of Bayou Chicot.) Document from Louisiana State Archives (St. Landry Parish, Donation Book, No. 192) provides evidence of Gilbert Sweat and his wife Frances donating land to Joseph Willis and the Calvary Baptist Church in Bayou Chicot on June 28, 1826. The author is descendant of Frances Sweat. Document was provided to the author by Jane Parker McManus.

Chapter One. The Meeting Place

1. Documents from the Louisiana State Archives show John Bass and his wife Delaney Bass in Louisiana by 1806. The 1810 census found in the Louisiana State Archives lists John Bass in St. Landry Parish as a "Free Person of Color."

2. The author possesses a copy of the original minutes of Amiable Baptist Church near Glenmora, Louisiana and founded in 1828. The minutes list John and Delaney Bass as founding members of Amiable Baptist Church on

September 6, 1828. They came from Bayou Chicot with the Rev. Joseph Willis to start Amiable Baptist Church. The minutes list John Bass as their first representative to the newly formed Louisiana Association of Baptist Churches.

3. Pearl Tippit Cooley, *Welcome Church of God – Established 1897*, from the Preface, Book Crafters (1997), v.

Chapter Four. Praying with a Forgiving Heart

1. Ibid., Louisiana State Archives Documents and Amiable Baptist Church Minutes.

2. Ibid., Amiable Baptist Church Minutes – August 21, 1830.

Chapter Five. Tearing Down Strongholds

1. Compilation by Leonard Allen, *The Contemporaries Meet the Classics on Prayer*, Howard Publishing (2003), 257.

2. William Gurnall, *The Christian in Complete Armor – Daily Readings in Spiritual Warfare*, Moody Press (1994), February 25.

Chapter Six. Desperate Praying

1. Pearl Cooley Tippit, Welcome Church of God, Preface.

2. Ibid.

3. Ibid.

4. Roy J. Fish, *When Heaven Touched Earth*, (Azle, Texas: Need of the Times Publishers), 299-324.

5. Ibid., 35.

Chapter Seven. Leaving a Legacy

1. Dictionary.com, an online dictionary.

2. Previously unpublished, here is a personal handwritten letter from Dr. Andrew Murray on August

30, 1913 to the Rev. Z. J. de Beer of Kalkbay, Cape Town, South Africa. The letter was transcribed by the Rev. Perold de Beer, grandson of the recipient; and permission was granted by the same to use the letter in this book.

MORE INFORMATION & RESOURCES

www.prayingforyourfamily.com

OTHER BOOKS BY SAMMY TIPPIT

The Prayer Factor

Light in the Darkness

Running Home

God's Secret Agent

Discover other books by Sammy Tippit at www.sammytippitbooks.com

---

Learn more about Sammy Tippit's international ministry and receive materials that help you to grow in Christ:

www.sammytippit.org

FOR MORE INFORMATION

Sammy Tippit Books
P.O. Box 781767
San Antonio, Texas, 78278
Phone: 1-210-492-7501
Email: **info@sammytippit.org**

Printed in Great Britain
by Amazon